Living in the Gap

Dennis J. Billy

Living in the Gap
Religious Life and the Call to Communion

New City Press
Hyde Park, New York

Published in the United States by New City Press
202 Comforter Blvd., Hyde Park, NY 12538
www.newcitypress.com
© 2011 Dennis J. Billy

Cover design by Durva Correia

Library of Congress Cataloging-in-Publication Data

Billy, Dennis Joseph.
  Living in the gap : religious life and the call to communion / Dennis J. Billy.
    p. cm.
  Includes bibliographical references.
  ISBN 978-1-56548-392-7 (pbk. : alk. paper) 1. Monastic and religious life.
2. Catholic Church—Doctrines. 3. Communities—Religious aspects—Catholic Church.
I. Title.
  BX2435.B485 2011
  248.8'94—dc23   2011021043

Printed in the United States of America

In memory of
my classmate, friend, and confrere
Rev. Dennis Joseph Demko, C.Ss.R.
(1952–2009)

"I ask not only on behalf of these,
but also on behalf of those who
will believe in me through their
word, that they may all be one.
As you, Father are in me and I am
in you, may they also be in us, so
that the world may believe that
you have sent me."

John 17:20–21

Contents

Abbreviations

CIC *Codex iuris canonici* [*Code of Canon Law*], Vatican City: Typis polyglottis Vaticanis, 1983. http://www.vatican.va/archive/ENG1104/_INDEX.HTM

LG Second Vatican Council, *Lumen gentium*, November 21, 1964. In *Decrees of the Ecumenical Councils* English ed., Norman Tanner, vol. 2 (London/Washington, D.C.: Sheed & Ward/Georgetown University Press, 1990), 849–900. http://www.vatican.va/archive/hist_councils/ii_vatican_council/documents/vat-ii_const_19641121_lumen-gentium_en.html.

NMI John Paul II, Apostolic Letter, *Novo millennio ineunete*, January 6, 2001. http://www.vatican.va/holy_father/john_paul_ii/apost_letters/documents/hf_jp-ii_apl_20010106_novo-millennio-ineunte_en.html.

PC Second Vatican Council, *Perfectae caritatis*, October 28, 1965. In *Decrees of the Ecumenical Councils* English ed., Norman Tanner, vol. 2 (London/Washington, D.C.: Sheed & Ward/Georgetown University Press, 1990), 939–47. http://www.vatican.va/archive/hist_councils/ii_vatican_council/documents/vat-ii_decree_19651028_perfectae-caritatis_en.html.

VC John Paul II, Post-Synodal Apostolic Exhortation, *Vita consecrata*, March 25, 1996. Vatican City: Libreria Editrice Vaticana, 1996. http://www.vatican.va/holy_father john_paul_ii/apost_exhortations/documents/hf_jp-ii exh_25031996_vita-consecrata_en.html.

Introduction

This book focuses on a vital topic for the life of the Church: the relationship between religious life and the "spirituality of communion." Religious are consecrated persons who, following Church law, live the common life and have made public vows of chastity, poverty and obedience (*CIC* 607.2). The "spirituality of communion," one of the most vibrant and visible expressions of Catholic spirituality in the post-Vatican II era, has its roots in the Biblical concept of *koinonía* (*communio* or "fellowship") and Jesus' prayer to his Father that "all may be one" (Jn 17:20–21). Although meant to be practiced by everyone, the "spirituality of communion" has particular significance for religious, since they are called to be "experts" in its daily practice. That is to say that they are to strive to implement it in the concrete circumstances of their everyday lives and encourage others to do the same.

Pope John Paul II offers one of the best descriptions of this spirituality. In practice, "[a] spirituality of communion indicates … the heart's contemplation of the mystery of the Trinity dwelling in us, and whose light we must also be able to see shining on the face of the brothers and sisters around us. A spirituality of communion also means an ability to think of our brothers and sisters in faith within the profound unity of the Mystical Body, and therefore as 'those who are a part of me.' This makes us able to share their joys and sufferings, to sense their desires and attend to their needs, to offer them deep and genuine friendship" (*NMI*, no. 43).

This way of thinking has a number of concrete implications:

A spirituality of communion implies the ability to see what is positive in others, to welcome it and prize it as a gift from God: not only as a gift for the brother or sister who has received it directly, but also as a "gift for me." A spirituality of communion means … to know how to "make room" for our brothers and sisters, bearing "each other's burdens' (Gal 6:2) and resisting the selfish temptations which constantly beset us and provoke competition, careerism, distrust, and jealousy. (*NMI*, no. 43)

Contemplating the other. Living in unity. Accepting each other as "gift." Sharing each other's burdens. It would be difficult to come up with a more comprehensive vision of living in right relationship with others. Communion, John Paul is saying, lies at the very heart of the Christian message. Living with God and one another in such a way is another way of talking about discipleship. To be a true disciple of Jesus Christ means living in communion with God and one another — without counting the cost.

Through these words, John Paul is inviting the faithful to be Christ's true disciples by contemplating the mystery of the Trinity within their hearts and discerning its presence in those around them. He asks them to be aware of the presence of others, to minister to their needs, and to reach out to them in a spirit of friendship. Doing so means making room for others in our lives and allowing them to make room for us. It means living in communion on every level of our human makeup: the physical, the emotional, the intellectual, the social, and the spiritual. The words of John Paul II describe a vision of "right relationship" that nearly everyone would embrace and few would fault or in any way disavow.

Difficulties in Religious Life

Most religious accept John Paul's vision of communion or right relationship. They find themselves genuinely inspired by this vision of authentic Christian discipleship. They get discouraged, however, by their inability to implement it. They identify closely with the words of St. Paul, "For I do not do the good I want, but I do the evil I do not want" (Rom 7:19). Walter Principe's distinction between the experiential, the doctrinal, and the analytical levels of spirituality also comes to mind.[1] If understood, the teaching on the "spirituality of communion" may easily be accepted as a vision to be implemented. It may even be studied, analyzed, and criticized so as to make it a more coherent body of teaching. On the experiential level, however, many have a difficult time making it an integral part of life. A gap, sometimes small and sometimes large, opens between the vision of what is professed and desired, and actual identity. Filling in that gap is necessary for fruitful personal, family, and community life.

John Paul II summons consecrated religious to be "true experts of communion" (*VC*, no. 46). Their desire for communion stems from being created in the image and likeness of the mysterious, personal, yet transcendent ground of love, the Trinity. Their call comes from Christ himself, the Second Person of the Trinity, who wants them to be

---

1. See Walter Principe, "Toward Defining Spirituality, *Studies in Religion/Sciences religieuses* 12(1983): 136; Michael Downey, ed. *The New Dictionary of Catholic Spirituality* (Collegeville, Minn.: The Liturgical Press, 1993), s.v. "Spirituality, Christian," by Walter H. Principe.

one just as he and his Father are one (Jn 10:30). They long for communion, but recognize that they are fallen and somewhat bent out of shape, dysfunctional creatures who have forgotten how to relate to each other, even as the imprint of the divinity continues to swell within and manifest itself in deepest longings. They yearn for communion with one another because of God's yearning for communion with each person. Although "out-of-step" with one another, they still hope that things can and will get better, not through personal effort, but because of the God who made us, loves us, and holds us in being.

Religious must face the truth: full communion among ourselves, others, and God can never be achieved at least in this life. The key question is not whether the gap between vision and experience exists in the lives of religious men and women, but whether they recognize it and assume responsibility for making it smaller and smaller. They need, in other words, to be able to recognize the gap, accept it as something that will never fully go away (at least in this life), and take appropriate steps to narrow it.

Purpose

This book attempts to refocus the discussion on the basics of religious life. Chapter one examines the language of conversion; chapter two follows with a brief study of the anthropology of the vows. Chapter three emphasizes the call to community, while chapter four examines the relevance of the "spirituality of communion" for religious. Chapter five underscores the importance of community structures for fostering a life of virtue, while chapter six looks to perseverance as an essential feature of contemporary religious life. Each of these chapters opens with an epigram about religious life and closes with a series of reflection questions. An epilogue poses questions and also issues a challenge to make religious life what it should be. A closing appendix discusses the various ways in which religious life has been compared to other states of life.

This book aims to root religious more firmly in their mission of living in communion with God, others, and the world around them. In doing so, it hopes to inspire them to be a leaven for the world so that they may be true messengers of the kingdom already their midst, yet still to come. As such, it seeks to remind them of the dignity of their call to leave all to follow Jesus in true Gospel fellowship and in unity of mind and heart.

1

The Language of Conversion

Every family or order is an "incarnation," so to speak, of an expression of Jesus, of an attitude of his, of an event of his life, of a suffering of his, of a word of his.... God loves every order insofar as it reflects his Son, the Idea of himself made human, Love "made flesh."

Chiara Lubich, "Church as Communion"[1]

To what extent do religious orders express the incarnation of Jesus? How do they represent attitudes, words, or events in his life? How do they express his love? Many cannot give genuine answers to such questions. This crisis goes beyond the breakdown of founding myths and resulting lack of purpose. Many — perhaps most — have some awareness that they have lost something of great importance for their lives as professed religious, but cannot describe what they have lost.

Confronted by an aging constituency, a steady exodus of younger members, and fewer and fewer vocational prospects, many have become disillusioned and look for

---

1. Chiara Lubich, "Church as Communion" in *Essential Writings: Spirituality, Dialogue, Culture* (Hyde Park, NY: New City Press, 2007), 113–14.

antidotes to their mounting misfortunes. These solutions take many forms. Some display nostalgia for the not too distant past. Many have resigned themselves to "inevitable corporate extinction." Others doubt the very relevance of religious life in the postmodern world. These responses to the crisis in religious life, however, are inadequate.

To move forward, religious congregations need not resign themselves to escape and denial. They can choose a language of conversion by which they can give an honest account of themselves, help them to integrate their private lives with their corporate existences, and show them how, together, they can respond to such doubts.

A Language of Conversion

This language of conversion speaks to the mind as well as to the heart. It satisfies intellectual longings and motivates individuals to examine their lives with renewed strength and vigor, with new eyes. More importantly, it reshapes experience so that, through the action of divine grace, they can recommit themselves to the charism of their particular order or congregation.

Without such conversion, individualism will corrode religious life; professed religious will lose faith in their corporate identities and fall into the "double life" syndrome that since the close of the Second Vatican Council has plagued many religious communities. The very future of religious life hangs in the balance.

Authentic conversion demands both individual and corporate change, particularly among those who have dedicated their lives to following the evangelical counsels. "The whole cannot be understood without its parts; nor the parts without the whole." A language of conversion must address the individual, the group, and their ongoing mutual relationship. To do so, however, it must contain certain key elements. It needs a sound Christian anthropology that stresses the existential dignity of the human person. It requires a philosophical "link" between the personal and the corporate wholes. Finally, those who use such a language must acknowledge its inherent limitations, and therefore leave themselves open to the recreative presence of God.

The Dimensions of Human Existence

What is "a sound Christian anthropology"? "Anthropology," the specific and coordinated assessment of human existence, is "Christian" insofar as it proceeds from the insights of Christian tradition. As there are numerous interpretations of the meaning of Christianity, there are also varying Christian anthropologies. A *sound* Christian anthropology integrates the fundamental dimensions of human existence — the physical, the mental (emotional as well as intellectual), the spiritual, and the social. St. Paul articulated such an anthropology in his doctrine of the Body of Christ (1Cor 12:12–31) and in the tripartite understanding of the person, as it is expressed in verses such as 1 Thes 5:23: "May the God of peace himself sanctify you entirely; and may your spirit (*pneuma*) and soul (*psyche*) and body (*soma*), be kept sound and blameless at the coming of our Lord Jesus Christ."

The spirit (*pneuma*) is the deepest part of a person's being. It yearns for God with unutterable groanings (Rom 8:22–23) and has the potential to be lifted up into intimate communion with the very Spirit of God. The human spirit affirms each person as *capax Dei*, i.e., capable of God. The soul (*psyche*), by way of contrast, is a person's animating principle of life. It encompasses not only the rational, but also the emotive, nutritive, and reproductive sides of human existence. Rational activity, the soul's highest and noblest function, enables a person to wonder about the meaning of life and to think critically about its problems. The body (*soma*) is the material extension of a person's existence. Unlike the term St. Paul uses for "flesh" (*sarx*), which has close associations with a life of sin leading to death, *soma* can be used for good *or* for ill, and hence is morally neutral. Finally, the social dimension is a constituent part a person's anthropological makeup. A human person arises out of and exists in a social context and cannot be understood apart from it. The primary social arena for Christians is the Body of Christ as it exists in its various local and universal expressions (e.g., the family, the parish, the diocese, the Church universal).

These dimensions of human existence are essentially interrelated. Spirit does not exist apart from a person's body, soul, and social relationships — and vice versa. Each dimension must be treated in relationship with the others; a person is not an artificial construct of composite and disparate parts. A continuous and unbroken anthropological relationship runs among *all* of them. Not even death can sever these bonds. To do so would mean the dissolution of the human person and the corresponding passage from being to non-being, a possibility of human destiny that Christian faith strongly rejects. Of course, there is a certain priority among these various anthropological factors. Spirit relates to soul as soul to body. Balanced and healthy relationships among these affect the way in which a person interacts with others. A sound social environment, in turn, produces healing effects on bodily, spiritual, and mental well-being. This reciprocal relationship has important repercussions for understanding what religious life should be. Its problems involve not only dysfunctional social structures, but also an imbalance of the deepest human relationships.

Uniting the Individual and Social Wholes

Social structures, which are produced by the mind, in turn shape intelligence and spirit. Structures that are just give each person his or her due and educate that person according to the way of virtue. Structures that are unjust benefit a privileged elite at the expense of an oppressed underclass and perpetuate a mentality of control that legitimizes the mistreatment of other human beings. Such structures are sinful and need to be changed. Doing so, however, can leave those who try to bring about change (as often it is in religious life) feeling overwhelmed at the immensity of the task before them. Such feelings can lead to a sense of helplessness or even indifference. A cycle of negativity can begin, in which individuals gradually lose ownership of their ruling structures, which in turn remain unchallenged more out of a paralyzing lack of interest than resistance to change.

One way to break this cycle is to introduce the related concepts of microcosm and macrocosm into the current vocabulary of religious life. Rooted in the Greek notion of the human person as a scale model of the cosmos, Plato adapted this distinction as a way of describing the relationship between individuals and society (see *Republic*, 441c). For Plato, the underlying structure of human society (the macrocosm) mirrors that of the human soul (the microcosm). The rational (or reasoning) element, for example, corresponds to the republic's governing class; the irascible (or spirited), to its military; the concupiscible (or sensual), to its productive masses. As "the human soul writ large," society offers individuals not only a particular place in the social hierarchy, but also the opportunity of seeing themselves projected onto the collective whole. Individuals find their reflection in the whole; the whole, in the individuals.

Not all of the Platonic model applies to religious life. His assertion, however, of an underlying structural continuity between individuals and the society to which they belong can be useful. It illustrates the reciprocal relationship between individual and social functions, the structural similarities between human subjects and their primary social environment, as well as the distinctiveness of the individual in the face of the larger community. Combining Platonic notions with a Christian anthropology offers a model by which individuals in religious communities can establish and maintain their sense of identity with the larger whole.

The physical, mental, spiritual, and social dimensions of the human person and the religious community resemble one another. The human spirit, for example, relates to the human soul *as* the community spirit relates to community soul. Such an analogy demonstrates a proportionate likeness and difference between the individual and society. An individual religious, in other words, should be able to see a reflection of himself or herself in the religious community to which he or she belongs — and vice versa. A member of the Missionaries of Charity, for example, should be able to see in her community a reflection of herself, as well as a reflection of the God in whose image and likeness she was made. This analogy maintains a fundamental continuity between the underlying anthropological structure of the individual and that of his or her religious community, even though language cannot really capture the quiet, abiding presence of God in the life of the community.

The Silence of Grace

Protracted theories can never replace the simplicity of God's intervening grace. Uneasiness about their lives has led many religious into a quest for "*the* perfect plan" that will explain why they find themselves in their present situation, how they can get themselves out of it, and where they should be going. No human theory, however, can satisfy such lofty expectations. A theory of refoundation or revitalization must place God at the center. Conversion on any level — the personal, the communal, the societal — comes directly from God's own initiative. Since God is not limited to human wisdom, theory can propose only one of the many possibilities for God's transforming action. By placing itself on the periphery (not at the center) of divine action, theory places itself more readily at the disposal of God's recreative activity.

"The wind blows where it chooses" (Jn 3:8). God's grace can transform both individuals and their social structures, but no one can foretell what God will do or how he will do it. In any of life's situations — including those that religious communities face — individuals and groups must recognize God working quietly in the circumstances of their daily lives. What is God saying in the graying of religious communities, in their steady loss of younger members, in their failure to attract vocations, and in their overall decline in numbers? Why does God permit a lack of identity and firmness of purpose in religious communities? Where is God leading, and to what purpose? The answer to such questions may not take the shape of a simple "yes" or "no." Trying to discover whether God is with a particular community or has abandoned it evades the real issue.

God's grace will foster a deep sense of listening in the life of a religious community. Most people want to speak their own opinion, and talk past those around them, tolerating what others say while looking for their next chance to talk. Conversation often devolves into a chain of vaguely connected monologues. Such is not the case with God — the listener *par excellence* — nor should it be for those stirred by the free gift of grace. Those who truly listen — to their own hearts, to those around them, to those in their community, and to those outside the community — can discern the voice of God in their own lives. When they nurture this quiet witness of faith, religious create a space in their community where others know that their presence will be recognized and their stories heard. Authentic followers of Christ empty themselves so others may be heard. The language of conversion cannot be spoken (let alone heard) outside the re-creative silence of God's transforming grace.

Religious and the Language of Conversion

An authentic language of conversion includes a sound Christian anthropology, a way of bringing together individual and corporate wholes, and a recognition of God's creative initiative in the process of conversion. By integrating these elements and using them as an active, functioning language, religious can find insight into their difficulties and discover the proper course of action to take. Taking such steps has positive consequences.

A language of conversion will challenge religious to move away from a mere "problem solving" mode of thinking. Rather than concentrating on what must be changed to secure institutional viability, they will focus on the authenticity of their religious lives. A religious community turns its life over to God not for ulterior motives (e.g., to get more vocations, to stem the exodus of disenchanted members), but simply because that is what God asks of them.

Religious will examine how they consider the relationship between "being" and "action." Informed by an anthropology that connects the physical, mental, spiritual, and social dimensions of human existence, they will recognize how their actions — both private and corporate — express their identity. The consequences of these actions resonate both inwardly and outwardly, shaping those who act and the world around them.

Religious must appreciate the basic human dimensions of community living. Membership in a religious congregation involves more than mere physical presence. It also entails a shared commitment to common goals and values, a general sense of how these ends are to be achieved, the fostering of community spirit, and a network of sound spiritual and social ties. Since these dimensions are intimately related, members must take care to relate well on all of them. Structures must be set in place to facilitate community life.

Particular emphasis should be given to the community's spiritual well-being. Just as the spirit is the deepest part of the human person — the part that yearns for God and affirms the human being as *capax Dei* ("capable of God") — it is also the most authentic part of the religious community. When the spirit of a religious community suffers, the other dimensions cannot help but be affected. The wounded spirit of religious community life must be healed. Among other things, this means working through issues such as human intimacy, vocational crises, members who leave or die, and dysfunctional or addictive behaviors. Only by healing the spirit of religious community life can members hope for recovery.

A community's wounded spirit can be healed by nurturing an atmosphere of genuine listening. By being attentive to the words of others — their stories and experiences — a person enters into the thick of life and allows God's presence to break into the ordinary course of daily events. An attitude of respect for those who wish to share themselves openly without feeling threatened allows a religious community to break out of dysfunctional ways of relating that keep its members trapped on a superficial level. One of the great failures of religious life is living for years without ever getting beyond a mere surface knowledge of each other.

A person in the religious life must develop a close intimate relationship with God. The language of conversion places God at the center. The purpose of life (particularly of religious life) is to enter into a deep and lasting friendship with God. Discussions about the future of religious life must place this basic purpose first. Religious vow to live the evangelical counsels in order to walk more closely along the way of the Lord Jesus. They do so in order to enter more closely into union with him and the one who sent him.

A person cannot know God if his or her spirit (or the spirit of the community, for that matter) does not commune with the Spirit of God through contemplation. The Lord must be sought in prayer. Without the incentive to pray, life becomes a meaningless going through the motions of living out evangelical commitments. Religious must maintain or retrieve the meaning of their religious life through a balanced regimen of prayer, gathering in God's name and continually invoking the divine presence.

Conversion takes place within a specific community environment. Religious must distribute their time appropriately between their own religious community and the people they serve in the apostolate. Strengthened by authentic sharing within their communities (an essential priority of a well-functioning community), they must then reach out beyond their immediate circle. The apostolic orientation of all religious communities (even strict contemplatives) must always remain a priority. The empowerment of religious by their communities will enable them — as individuals and as a whole — to do great work for the Church and for society.

Conclusion

Western philosophy has always struggled to resolve the problem of the relationship between one and the many. Those in religious life face the same tension. Over the years, the pendulum has swung from the extreme of the individual being subsumed into the collective whole (often the case prior to the Second Vatican Council) to the extreme of being increasingly removed from it (as often occurred after the Council). A healthy balance somehow needs to be struck, but there is no consensus concerning how to achieve it.

This chapter used categories from Western religious and philosophical traditions in order to suggest how religious communities might achieve this balance. These categories include: a Pauline anthropology that emphasizes the basic dimensions of human existence (i.e., the spiritual, mental, bodily, and social), a philosophical "link" between the individual and corporal wholes (as found in the distinction of ancient Greek philosophers between microcosm and macrocosm), and an awareness of the inherent limitations of language (and by extension theory) with a corresponding focus on the creative initiative of divine grace. General discourse concerning religious life has touched upon these categories, but rarely have they been used in conjunction with one another, certainly not in the context of "a language of conversion."

Through these categories of conversion, religious can refresh or restructure their ways of relating and allow their wounds to heal. The call to conversion extends to individuals, but also their social structures. The next chapter addresses this important anthropological question. An awareness of the reciprocal relationship between the human heart and human social structures must precede any serious discussion of religious life.

Reflection Questions

How would your founder or foundress see your religious order? Would he or she be happy with it or saddened by it? What concrete changes would he or she seek? What would he or she do differently today from the time of the order's founding? What would you do to implement your founder's vision more effectively on the universal, provincial, and local levels? Does it relate in any way to developing an authentic language of conversion? If so, how?

2

An Anthropology of the Vows

"What would become of the world if there were no Religious?" Beyond all superficial assessments of its usefulness, the consecrated life is important precisely in its being *unbounded generosity and love*, and this all the more so in a world which risks being suffocated in the whirlpool of the ephemeral. "Without this concrete sign there would be a danger that the charity which animates the entire Church would grow cold, that the salvific paradox of the Gospel would be blunted, and that the 'salt' of faith would lose its savor in a world undergoing secularization." The Church and society itself need people capable of devoting themselves totally to God and to others for the love of God.

John Paul II, *Vita consecrata*[1]

Religious show the world what it means to be human. People look to them to get a sense of the sacred and to see the moral and spiritual values that lead to a full life. That is not to say that everyone should dress or act like

---

1. John Paul II, *Vita consecrata*, no. 105.

them. They should, however, experience in the religious a sense of what it means to live a good and virtuous life. The four pillars of religious life — chastity, poverty, obedience, community life — not only point to the beyond, but represent how to live in the here-and-now.

In *Vita consecrata*, his post-synodal apostolic exhortation on the consecrated life, Pope John Paul II writes of "the profound anthropological significance of the counsels" (*VC*, no. 87). He does so when speaking about the prophetic stance of consecrated life in the challenges that the Church faces. In this important statement, the pope points out how the vows can deepen and even transform self-understanding. This chapter draws out the implications of this key anthropological statement.

The Right Question

How the vows are understood and lived reflects how human beings view themselves and their world. This has always been true, even when the Church's understanding of the vows was much different than it is today. At one time, for example, the counsels were seen as a way of rising above the material dimension of human existence and to escape the bonds of the physical world — including sexuality. Lives of perfect chastity, poverty, and obedience were thought to lead to a higher plane of existence, one which enabled the religious to overcome bodily passions and be free of otherwise normal attachments to family, possessions, and self-will.

Such a conception of the counsels stemmed from an underlying ethical dualism manifested most pointedly in distrust of the body and the bodily passions. This deep-seated suspicion was galvanized by Augustine's explanation of original sin, which condemned the Gnostic equation of matter with evil yet maintained a close association between sin and sexual intercourse. Such an estimation of the body and bodily passion (what Augustine called "concupiscence"), filtered through the Church's historical memory, still maintains a subtle influence on how the counsels are understood. This is so even though current theological understanding of the vows and of the doctrine of original sin itself is guided by anthropological assumptions that differ decidedly from those of Augustine's era.

Every theology of the counsels is rooted in underlying anthropological assumptions. The more we are aware of them, the better we can discern whether they express our own self-understanding. The counsels always have had profound anthropological significance. The question that ought to be posed concerning at any particular stage in the Church's history, past or present, is: "*Which* anthropology and *what* significance are we talking about?"

Vita Consecrata

In *Vita consecrata*, John Paul II describes the anthropological significance of vows:

> The decision to follow the counsels, far from involving an impoverishment of truly human values, leads instead to their transformation. The evangelical counsels should not be considered as a denial of the values inherent in sexuality, in the legitimate desire to possess material goods or to make decisions for oneself. Insofar as these inclinations are based on nature, they are good in themselves. Human beings, however, weakened as they are by original sin, run the risk of acting on them in a way which transgresses the moral norms.

The profession of chastity, poverty and obedience
is a warning not to underestimate the wound of
original sin and while affirming the value of created
goods, it *relativizes them* by pointing to God as the
absolute good. Thus, while those who follow the
evangelical counsels seek holiness for themselves,
they propose, so to speak, a spiritual "therapy" for
humanity, because they reject idolatry of anything
created and in a certain way they make visible the
living God. The consecrated life, especially in difficult times, is a blessing for human life and for the
life of the Church. (87)

This passage affirms the fundamental goodness of
human sexuality, material possessions, and human
freedom. At the same time, it recognizes the capacity
of each human being to abuse these basic goods, even
to idolize them. The evangelical counsels put these
goods into proper perspective by referring them to God,
the absolute good of human life, thus diminishing the
exaggerated worth that may be assigned to them. This
process provides a "spiritual therapy" which, through the
operation of grace, heals people's wounds and transforms
human values. By invoking God as the absolute good to
which the counsels point, the pope puts human existence
in proper perspective. It is not an end in itself but is actually
oriented beyond itself. By looking beyond themselves,
human beings can discover their truest, deepest meaning.

In this presentation, John Paul II affirms five fundamental points. All creation is fundamentally good. Although
weakened by the effects of original sin, human nature
is not totally corrupted. God, who is all-good, alone is
worthy of praise and adoration. The vows point toward
the ultimate aim of human existence, and their anthropological orientation accounts for their therapeutic (i.e.,

healing) and transformative (i.e., elevating) effect. These theological and anthropological affirmations demonstrate how the counsels are to be understood and assimilated. They remind us that we are wounded creatures capable of being healed and elevated by the truly plentiful grace of redemption.

John Paul II also notes three major challenges that the Church must face and the prophetic role of consecrated life in responding to each of them. The first is "a *hedonistic culture* which separates sexuality from all objective norms, often treating it as a mere diversion and a consumer good and, with the complicity of the means of social communication, justifying a kind of idolatry of the sexual instinct" (88). Through their lives of chastity, consecrated persons respond to such cultural tendencies by showing that it is possible "to love God with all one's heart, putting him above every other love, and thus to love every creature with the freedom of God" (88). The second is "a *materialism which craves possessions*, heedless of the needs and sufferings of the weakest, and lacking any concern for the balance of natural resources" (89). Consecrated persons' lives of evangelical poverty attest "that God is the true wealth of the human heart" which "forcefully challenges the idolatry of money, making a prophetic appeal as it were to society, which in so many parts of the developed world risks losing the sense of proportion and the very meaning of things" (89). The third "comes from those *notions of freedom* which separate this fundamental human good from its essential relationship to the truth and moral norms" (91). Consecrated persons respond to this through a life which "reproposes the obedience of Christ to the Father and ... testifies *that there is no contradiction between obedience and freedom*" (91). Consecrated persons, in other words, respond to the challenges that the Church faces through lives dedicated to the evangelical counsels. They do so not alone, but in community, "the particular sign, before Church and society, of the bond which comes from the same call and the common desire — notwithstanding differences of race and origin, language and culture — to be obedient to that call" (92). Life in community helps consecrated men and women to live the counsels, and signals the true ends toward which both Church and society are tending — the kingdom that is, at one and the same time, already here and yet to come.

Further Integration

The insights of John Paul II into the anthropological dimensions of the consecrated life and its prophetic response to the challenges that the Church faces are only a beginning. Further development of his fundamental insights is possible and even necessary for a more thorough understanding of the vows. This development explores the fundamental anthropological dimensions of human existence: the physical, the emotional, the intellectual, the spiritual, and the social.

The Physical. The counsels make sense only if they have a concrete, physical expression. They are easy to talk about, but much more difficult to live out in the concrete circumstances of life. The physical, bodily expressions of vows must be taken seriously. Consecrated persons are called to be chaste, to be poor, to be obedient — and this should be obvious by the lives they lead. It is easy, however, to fall into the trap of self-deception, to rationalize compromises with the counsels and end up being chaste, poor and obedient in name only. Religious are called to much more than that.

The Emotional. The physical expression of the counsels would be cold and meaningless if not heartfelt. Emotions, although complex and sometimes threatening, must be integrated into a life dedicated to the counsels. Otherwise, religious may well end up leading double lives, where their outward actions do not correspond with their deepest feelings and emotions. It is a mistake for institutes of consecrated life to repress or ignore this dimension of human existence. Like anyone else, consecrated persons need to learn how to deal with their emotions — those which help them to deepen their commitment, as well as those which could weaken it — and integrate them into their life commitments. Consecrated persons who have not learned how to integrate their emotions into their lives are often unhappy people who make other people unhappy and who find community difficult.

The Intellectual. The counsels demand regular reflection — by individuals and by the group. Consecrated persons need to keep abreast of psychology and the social sciences, particularly developments that help with deepening the understanding of their charism within the Church. Since the Second Vatican Council, the theology of the counsels has changed and will continue to do so. Reflecting upon the meaning of the counsels, reading what theologians and spiritual writers are saying about them, discussing them in community facilitates the integration of spiritual commitments with the rest of life. Consecrated persons need creativity in their witness to the world through the counsels. Theological reading, reflection, and conversation insure that they grasp new ideas and express them in their lives and ministry. Religious cannot learn everything they need to know about the vows during novitiate. Continuing education is a lifelong process.

The Spiritual. Consecrated persons need to be still and allow their spirits to yearn for God. In the deepest dimension of the self, the Spirit of God communes with their own spirits and they can find strength for living the vowed life. By professing the evangelical counsels, they seek to follow Jesus. This life of imitation involves an intimate relationship with the Spirit of Jesus which propels them to live the way he did, and to do so with all their heart, mind, soul, and strength. Consecrated people need to be men and women of contemplation. There are many forms of prayer and each person and each community favors one or another. Every form, however, can lead to contemplation. Being still and listening, allowing one's spirit to yearn, to groan, to breathe, gives prayer its proper emphasis and helps in living the counsels. Contemplation tames the deep, inordinate passions that are part of fallen human nature, integrating them into the rest of life. Through contemplation, human spirits gradually become chaste, poor, and obedient to the movements of the Holy Spirit. Contemplation allows religious to live "in the Spirit" and to see how the vows fit in to such a life.

The Social. Vows are lived individually as well as in community. Consecrated persons need close, intimate friends with whom they feel free and secure enough to share their problems and difficulties. They also need a wider circle of friends and acquaintances. Most of all, they need community. Human beings learn about themselves and become who they are called to be through social interaction. Learning the meaning of the counsels and receiving help to live them in the same manner. Consecrated persons are oriented toward community life because the counsels themselves are rooted in a communal understanding of human existence. The social dimensions of consecrated life give meaning to being chaste, poor, obedient. This holds true even for the hermit, who lives alone, but whose life and actions lay hidden in the contemplative heart of the Church.

Although equally important, each of these dimensions is understood and incorporated into life in different degrees. People differ in terms of personality, family background, and cultural origins, as well as in levels of education, religious training, and the traditions of the community to which they belong. To lead an integrated life, consecrated persons should pay attention and give appropriate expression to each of these dimensions.

Conclusion

John Paul II's emphasis on the anthropological dimensions of the counsels reveals the challenge *beneath* the challenges that consecrated persons in the Church must face. The counsels must penetrate *every* dimension of life, not only those most convenient or accommodating to personal needs. A true prophetic response to worldly hedonism, materialism, and individualism in the world today depends upon living the counsels in all of their dimensions — the physical, the emotional, the intellectual, the spiritual, and the social. Living them in any other way compartmentalizes the counsels, allowing them to take shape in one or more areas of life, but not transforming it completely. Religious people will not be taken seriously because they do not take themselves seriously.

Reflecting on the counsels across these five dimensions reveals the depth of their anthropological significance. The goodness of creation, for example, extends not only to physical well-being, but to the emotional, the intellectual, the spiritual, and the social as well. All of these dimensions, moreover, have been weakened by humanity's primordial fall but are placed in their proper position when seen in relationship to God as the Absolute Good. All have an eschatological significance and all are healed and elevated by God's plentiful redeeming grace. The counsels reveal the true significance of human existence by placing the whole of life in perspective, by demonstrating its radical dependence on God. This is what consecrated persons give witness to, live their lives for, and die for. In the next chapter, we will see what this means for their life in community.

Reflection Questions

What do the evangelical counsels have to do with the various dimensions of human existence? What does life in religious community have to do with them? How do the counsels relate to our basic human makeup? To what extent are they related to the prophetic and eschatological stance of religious in the world today? What would the world be like without religious? What would the world be like without your religious order?

3

Called to Community

If our brother and sister are the "sacrament" of
meeting with Christ, if love is the Christian's "way,"
if in the mutuality of love there is the possibility of
experiencing the Trinitarian God, then the community is the privileged place for living the Christian
vocation in all its fullness.

Fabio Ciardi, *Koinonia*[1]

To say — at least among Catholics — that the call to
discipleship includes community rarely elicits disagree-
ment. Whatever their calling (priest, religious, or lay), most
recognize the importance of community in the journey of
faith. Simple agreement, however, does not always signify
understanding; it may even prevent deeper examination
of what is taken for granted. How many, for example,
understand the call to "community" as being at the very
center of a response to God? How many are aware that
life in community is intrinsic to a relationship with God,
that community leads to the very mystery of who God is?
And how many actually acknowledge such ideas in day-

---

1. Fabio Ciardi, *Koinonia: Spiritual and Theological Growth of the Religious Community* (Hyde Park, NY: New City Press, 2001), 323.

to-day circumstances? Reflecting on the call to community can enhance how to discern and live out the vocation to discipleship.

Vision and Call

Everyone needs a vision in life. Call it a dream or a purpose; call it a goal, or a sense of direction; call it a founding myth or a narrative of origins; whatever it is called, everyone needs a way to make sense out of experience and to share it with others. Christian community maintains such a vision and supports the concrete steps needed to pursue it in everyday life. It keeps life's larger context in focus and connects those who are part of it with the traditions that have shaped them and which, to a large degree, have made them who they are. It also challenges them to confront the dark side of human experience and to remain steadfast in their response to God's call.

Communities vary in size and shape because they respond to different needs within the Church and reflect the variety of God's creation. Families and base communities, parishes and religious congregations, secular institutes and third order sodalities flourish when they correspond to the purpose for which they were founded. Community is not peripheral to God's call, as if to say its purpose is to provide an atmosphere conducive to private personal spiritual growth or to respond to some human need. Christian community can and does provide for such things. It is meant, however, to be and to do much more. Life in community is intrinsic to the journey into the mystery of God. The Christian vocation requires community. It loses purpose and conviction outside the context of a call; entering into the divine mystery is inherently communal. Christian community and Christian vocation enjoy a close, reciprocal relationship. It is impossible to have one without the other.

The term "vocation" here refers not to a specific state in life in the Church (i.e., religious, priestly, or lay), but to the fundamental call to intimate friendship that God extends to everyone, believer and non-believer alike. This call to beatitude (or to the "beatific vision" as theologians used to call it) extends to all people, regardless of their faith, nationality, race, or position in life. It underscores the capacity of every person to be lifted up through grace and to see God face-to-face. This universal, mystical vocation is forged and nurtured through life in community. Because God's nature is inherently communal, the call to divine friendship is established and perfected through a life lived with and oriented towards others.

The Trinitarian Community

The Christian tradition acclaims God as the perfect community of love. God who has conceived of us, who has created us, and who holds us in being relates to us in a manner proportionate to his nature. God who is love cannot but relate to us in love. Although the doctrine of the Trinity is vast and intricate, it is enough to say that, however God's mystery of intimate social relations is described — as Father-Son-Spirit, or as Creator-Redeemer-Sanctifier, or as Ground- Other-Bond — the very nature of the Godhead consists in the mutual indwelling of persons. Although no single formulation can convey the inexhaustible meaning and depth of the mystery of God, revelation teaches that God, a single being of three clearly differentiated relations, is communal. From this perspective, union with God becomes a never-ending journey into the intimate community of divine relationships.

This may sound distant and unrelated to the daily concerns of Christian community. Lofty ideas about the Trinity may seem to have little practical value in the nitty-gritty tensions and concerns of communal living. The Trinity, however, is the ultimate reality from which all else follows as a consequence. The Trinity is *the quintessential fact*. It is not simply a metaphor, or a purely human construct, or a projection of the deepest human hopes onto a divine plane. God's self-disclosure to humanity as Trinity is a divinely revealed truth. The intimate community who is God and who human beings call the Trinity is the alpha and omega, the beginning and end of all things. The Trinity is the goal of human existence, the force that directs human life on earth, the reality that draws human beings to their final destiny.

Through life in Christian community, God prepares human beings to participate in the mystery of triune love. If it is true, as St. Augustine and many medieval thinkers proposed, that God has imprinted traces of the divine nature in the very fabric of creation, then life in Christian community is a reflection of God's hidden presence in the world. No one could be ready or even capable of sharing in the intimate relations of the divine nature without long preparation. Most need to be led, step by step, along the long and narrow way of the Lord. Christian community, one might say, is the fiery forge in which God tempers personalities and gets them ready to share more deeply in the fullness of the divine community. It stretches character, challenging individuals to take others into account.

To use an example from the Catholic mystical tradition, it *purges* imperfections, *illumines* the journey through life, and eventually leads to a state of *union* with God. Life in community helps individuals to discover and become their truest, deepest selves; it naturally overflows in relationship with others; it shows precisely what it means to be friends of God. Community life gives a taste of God's triune love. The deeper it is entered, the more it prepares persons for relationship with God — during earthly life, and in the life to come. Christian community, *koinonia*, is fellowship of God's friends; it is "church." First formed by Jesus himself and walking forever in his way, this circle of close disciples perpetuates itself by forging genuine human relationships.

The Way of Jesus

If the Trinitarian basis of Christian community seems too remote from day-to-day living, a more concrete example comes from the life of Jesus himself. The gospels show him always calling people to fellowship, especially outcasts. He welcomed prostitutes and tax collectors, the poor and the possessed, the blind and the lame to partake in the friendship he shared with the Father. His gathering of disciples, his preaching through parables, his emphasis on table fellowship, his institution of the Eucharist in the context of a meal, all reveal his deep concern to provide others with a sense of God's gratuitous love and care for them. Jesus reached out to others because they were children of the Father, and needed God's friendship (see Jn 15:15).

Jesus' call to fellowship continues. Then, as now, it is the perfect expression of the Son's intimate love of the Father. His entering the world (the incarnation), giving of himself completely (dying for us), becoming our very food and nourishment (Eucharist), and being the source of hope (the Resurrection) express the same selfless giving that makes up the life of the Trinity. Jesus' love for humanity reveals the love which he shares with his Father in an even deeper way. Their intimate relationship enables him to listen to the Father's concerns as a loyal and faithful Son. His humble response manifests the self-diffusive nature of God's love and discloses why Christ came into the world, lived in service of others, was crucified, rose from the dead, ascended into heaven, and will one day return in glory.

Jesus' life provides an ideal vision of life in community. Just as Christ entered the world and gave himself completely, so too are Christians, as individuals and in community, called to enter the worlds of people around them. They are to give themselves in service to others as Jesus did, to the point of being nourishment and a source of life-giving hope. This calling reveals the fundamental meaning of Christian identity. It is not accomplished alone, but in cooperation with Christ and through the grace of his Spirit.

The Eucharist makes this process of divinization concrete and visible. There, Christians gather as "church" around the table of the Lord and pray to the Father, through the Son and in the Spirit. There, they celebrate the fellowship of God's friends by reenacting Jesus' last meal on earth and his sacrificial death the following day. There, they welcome the risen Lord not only in their hearts and in their midst, but in the very food they eat and drink. There, they celebrate the gift of "God among them" and recognize, in the breaking of the bread, that they are called to become other Christs and to radiate his presence in their lives (see Mt 18:20).

Practical Realities

These Trinitarian and Christological bases for life in community do not automatically bring about growth in the Spirit. As members of Christ's body, Christians recognize their calling to share in God's love and to carry on Christ's mission through time. They also recognize, however, that human limitations and self-centered concerns prevent them from living up to their vocation. Sin — original, social, personal — distracts people from their mission and leads them into compromises that fragment their vision and separate it from daily life. These downfalls, however, are the precise places where the community can review and restore its calling.

Vision. A Christian community must keep in view its charism, its reason for existence. Vision requires both head and heart. Community may begin through intellectual assent to the values and goals that called it into existence, but it must maintain a vision that seizes the members' imagination and generates the desire to make their objectives real. For this reason, Christian communities need inspired dreamers who remind everyone of their founding vision, as well as prudent leaders who can interpret this vision in the practical contexts of daily life. Without vision, the community will lose focus, scatter its energies, and eventually die out.

Structures. Every community needs order. Structures give the community stability, durability, and continuity. Without ongoing scrutiny, however, a community can find its structures losing relevance, inhibiting relationships and upsetting the tranquility necessary to fulfill its purpose. Every community, therefore, needs to examine its structures periodically, changing those that no longer serve their purpose or that obstruct its members' lives. No community is perfect but one — the Holy Trinity itself — so structures need constant scrutiny to ensure that they truly respond to community needs and goals.

Interaction. Communities need to interact with the world around them. If they concern themselves mainly with their own affairs, they risk losing touch with reality and their ability to make sound, prudent decisions. Communities that define themselves in terms of opposition to the world cut themselves off from it. For this reason, a community needs to complement its valid concern to define itself with efforts to open itself to, dialogue with, and engage those outside it. In a healthy community, members offer hospitality and service to those in need. At the same time, they take care not to fall into the opposite extreme, becoming so absorbed in external activities that they lose touch with the inner life that propels the community and gives its actions meaning.

Individuality. Authentic community life consists in a balanced relationship between the community and its individual members. The community must respect its members' personal lives so as to assure their psychological health and stability. Individual members must respect the community's valid claims upon them so as to assure its social viability and corporate existence. When Christian communities (of whatever kind) highlight the complementary relationship between individuals and their corporate identity, they acknowledge the dignity of the human person in the context of community, mediating the world to individuals and allowing individuals the freedom to respond.

Personality. Through its variety of "personality types" — be they as described in categories according to Jung or Myers-Briggs, or even the Enneagram — a community has a rich resource of human strengths and talents. Such variety can and will bring about conflict; but conflict presents an opportunity for growth. Community members need not be confidants or friends. They should, however, subsume their differences in outlook and taste for the common good of the community. Such selfless efforts are valuable. Christ exhorted his disciples to "Love your enemies and pray for those who persecute you, so that you may be children of your Father in heaven" (Mt 5:44). At the very least, even if they do not always get along, community members should be kind to one another.

Intimacy. When it develops, community members should recognize and welcome the divine gift of friendship. Close friends, however, should keep their relationship open to others, lest it divide the life of the community. This is part of the reason why many religious communities traditionally discourage particular friendships. Friends who are members of the same community should reflect on the meaning of their relationship. Do they contribute to the life of the community? Do they detract from its goals and purposes? Do they make time and room for others, inviting them to participate in their activities and reflections? Such questions can help friends avoid forming cliques, but even more importantly can guide them to contribute greatly to community life.

Motivation. Members may have different reasons for joining and continuing to belong to a community. These may include family history, economic concerns, educational interests, career choices, or social or psychological needs. Leaders should recognize such mixed motivations and help members become aware of them. The more such motivations are understood and dealt with, the more members can focus their energy on what the community as a whole states and professes.

Involvement. Community members need to feel that their contribution counts and makes a difference in the life of the community. Without this sense of involvement, they may slip away from the spirit of the group into non-committal or passive-aggressive behavior, or indifference. Members who display indifference to the life and goals of the community should be asked to explain their behavior. Sometimes, a deeper issue is not being addressed either by the individual or the group. If deeper issues are not surfaced and addressed, the community risks more and more of its members succumbing to the awkward and painful situation of deliberate uninvolvement. It is always better to act proactively, lest such situations influence the entire community.

Awareness. Members need to be aware of the particular needs of their community. Such awareness requires sensitivity to the needs of the group, to differing assumptions about the division of labor, and openness to those responsible within the community. Even seemingly insignificant actions can have an effect on the larger community. Being aware of such details of community living and deciding to do something about them personally creates an atmosphere of participation that will serve the community well in larger, more significant situations. Members who pay attention to the small details of community living insure the smooth running of its internal affairs and contribute to the realizing of its larger purposes and goals.

Loneliness. Community life always includes a certain degree of loneliness, but being alone need not be negative. Such feelings can lead to a healthy integration of experience. Just because members live and even work together does not necessarily mean that they relate to one another beyond superficial levels. Healthy community life requires a willingness to delve beneath the surface and to share the experiences and concerns which really matter. Members need to channel their loneliness into an atmosphere of trust where they feel free to relate the pain in their personal lives and in the life of the community.

While Christian communities must never lose sight of the vision that calls them into being and sustains their continued existence, they must also deal with the practical (sometimes painful) realities of everyday life. Those who can integrate these two aspects of the same call will understand more deeply the nature of God's presence in human history and how he continues to work and act in their midst.

Conclusion

The call to community is not peripheral to Christian life, but an essential ingredient of the common human journey into the mystery of God. An authentic Christian community must be sustained by a Trinitarian and Christological vision and, at the same time, be flexible enough to deal with the practical, everyday difficulties that will surely arise. Both elements are crucial. If it focuses solely on vision, a community may develop unrealistic expectations of what it can do. If it focuses solely on practical matters, it may give up trying to make it a better place to live. With both, a community keeps its vision before it, while taking prudent steps for improving the quality of its life and witness.

This twofold focus of vision and practical reality comes together through the call to conversion. Community must keep before themselves the one *perfect* community — the Trinity itself. Not living up to that vision which they profess should not cause discouragement or (worse yet) depression. Failure is an invitation to change. "Convert us Lord and we will be converted" (Lam 5:21). Few can turn their lives around completely through their own efforts. They need the help and encouragement of others and the grace of God to change their hearts and fill them with the desire to conform their lives to his will. The call to conversion brings together the concrete reality of who they are, and the vision of what they one day hope to become. The call to conversion highlights both facets of the call to community and issues a reminder that change will come about only in those who are docile to the Spirit and open to the initiative of God.

Finally, a community of conversion, first and foremost, must be a community of prayer. A Christian community must turn to God for help in sustaining its vision and coping with its shortcomings. Substantial changes in the quality of a community's life and witness come about by members praying together and lifting up each other's needs, asking the Lord to change their hearts and help them to overcome their weaknesses. If community members pray together for the humility to accept the truth and to acknowledge their failures, if they ask for the courage to forgive those who have hurt them and to approach those whom they have hurt, if they ask God to make them generous with their time and open with their lives and willingness to share, then they will already be well on their way to experiencing the mystery of God befriending them where they are and helping them, as a group, to enter more deeply into the divine mystery. The call to community manifests itself as a call to conversion, which itself becomes a call to a deeper life of prayer. Prayer carries human beings to their destiny in God. With prayer, there is nothing to fear and everything to hope for. This applies to religious in a special way. Since their very call seeks to turn them into "true experts of communion," practical knowledge of the "spirituality of communion" must flow both into and from the heart of their life and mission.

Reflection Questions

Why is community life intrinsic to the call to discipleship? How does it help a community to remain steadfast to God's call in their lives? What specific challenges does community life present to the life of religious and their attempt to give concrete expression to the Gospel message? What effect does it have on the public witness of the vows of poverty, chastity, and obedience? What can a community do to make its witness of the vows more visible?

4

The Spirituality of Communion

During his earthly life, the Lord Jesus called those whom he wished in order to have them at his side and to train them to live, according to his example, for the Father and for the mission which he had received from the Father (cf. *Mk* 3:13–15). He thus inaugurated the new family which down the centuries would include all those ready to "do the will of God" (cf. *Mk* 3:32–35). After the Ascension, as a result of the gift of the Spirit, a fraternal community formed around the Apostles, gathered in the praise of God and in a concrete experience of communion (cf. *Acts* 2:42–47; 4:32–35). The life of that community and, even more, the experience of complete sharing with Christ lived out by the Twelve, have always been the *model to which the Church has looked* whenever she has sought to return to her original fervor and to resume with fresh evangelical vigor her journey through history.

John Paul II, *Vita consecrata*[1]

1. John Paul II, *Vita consecrata*, 41.

"Koinonia" or "Communio" lies at the very heart of the Church's life and message. It has its roots in Jesus' relationship with his disciples and the Church's experience of the Spirit at Pentecost. This chapter looks into the origins of the "spirituality of communion," sums up its principal characteristics, and highlights its importance for religious, especially as manifested in the thought of the late Pope John Paul II.

Origins and Characteristics of Communion

The "spirituality of communion" flows from the very heart of the Trinity, where the Father, Son, and Holy Spirit exist in a timeless community of mutual love and respect. By its very nature this community is "self-diffusive" — it freely goes out of itself to express its love. This happens most notably in the act of creation, when, led by the Father, the three Persons of the Trinity bring into existence the universe and all that inhabit it.

The apex of God's creative action was making man and woman in his own image and likeness. Its nadir was humanity's fall from grace instigated by the evil one, who convinced man and woman to place *themselves* at the center of the universe rather than God. Humanity's fall had a cataclysmic effect on all of God's creation, introducing imbalance and hostility into a cosmos created for order and harmony. Because of the Fall, human beings have a wild and unruly nature, a tendency toward sin (concupiscence), sickness and death, weakness of mind, will, and heart, as well as fragmentation and dispersion through the multiplication of languages. These are nothing, however, in comparison with the loss of grace and fellowship with God, all a consequence of pride, whereby humanity, tempted by the evil one, set itself up to be like God.

From the outset God envisioned the Fall but allowed it anyway for a greater good — *to have a world that would one day love him back*. For this to happen, however, he had to create beings with the capacity to receive his love and return it. He achieved this by creating angels and human beings with free will. According to Church tradition, Michael the Archangel and heavenly hosts turned their intuitive natures entirely to God. Lucifer and the fallen angels refused and convinced humanity (Adam and Eve) to follow suit, enticing them with the lure of knowing good and evil, which would make them like gods.

Seeing the possibility (even probability) of creation's fall, at the very outset God devised a threefold plan. Creation, led by the Father, would be followed by redemption, led by the Son, which would be followed by sanctification, led by the Spirit. This plan would not only reestablish order and harmony in creation, but elevate it, enabling humanity to participate even more deeply in the intimate communion of divine love. God's creative, redemptive, and sanctifying powers flow from his very being and are oriented toward the mission of communion. This means that the spirituality of communion has Trinitarian, Christological, and Pneumatic dimensions that are independent of creation (by reason of God's nature) yet intimately tied to it (by reason of God's plan).

From these dimensions, moreover, emerge the Ecclesial and Marian dimensions, whereby the Church, born of the Spirit, heralds the establishment of the new creation on earth with the Blessed Mother as the first human to experience the fullness of communion with the Trinitarian God through the merits of her Son's paschal mystery. In this light, it is clear how the spirituality of communion emerges from a multifaceted way of looking at life. Those who embrace the spirituality of communion point to these various dimensions of divine love in their work to establish the new creation of God on earth.

Issuing from the intimate life of the Trinity and the kenotic self-emptying of Christ in his incarnation and paschal mystery, the spirituality of communion has important repercussions for life in the Spirit and for every dimension of Christian theology and spirituality. The spirituality of communion flows from the very being of the Trinity itself. In *The Trinity: Life of God, Hope for Humanity*, Thomas J. Norris identifies its elements: the capacity to relate to others, the ability to reciprocate love, the experience of mutual indwelling or "living in another," the ability to empty oneself for the sake of another (as in Christ's double kenosis of the incarnation and the cross), and living in unity in the midst of diversity.[2] Jesus himself lived these values when he walked the earth and wanted his disciples to do the same. As Fabio Ciardi points out in *Koinonia*: "To become true disciples and form Jesus' authentic community, the Twelve will have to walk behind him, enroll in his school, assimilate his wisdom, and imitate those profound attitudes by which Jesus communicates the divine agape. In the Master's school, the community of the Twelve must become what it is meant to be."[3] During their earthly sojourn, however, the community of disciples will always be a "community in the making," in need of *metanoia*, the continual process of conversion to mutual, selfless love. Chiara Lubich, the founder of the Focolare Movement and one of the major proponents of the spirituality of communion, cites conversion to this communitarian dimension as one of its more original charac-

---

2. Adapted from the characteristics of Trinitarian Ontology in Thomas J. Norris, *The Trinity: Life of God, Hope for Humanity. Towards a Theology of Communion* (Hyde Park, NY: New City Press, 2009), 157–64.

3. Ciardi, *Koinonia*, 30.

teristics.[4] She also points to mutual love as a key value of this "new spirituality" and emphasizes the cost of "reciprocal love" through "daily training and sacrifice."[5] She perceives an intimate relationship between the spirituality of the cross ("Jesus Forsaken") and the spirituality of communion ("Jesus in Our Midst"): "Nothing good, useful or fruitful is accomplished in the world without knowing how to accept fatigue and suffering, in a word, the cross."[6] Lubich also emphasizes the universal dimensions of the spirituality of communion: "This communitarian spirituality," she holds, "is not exclusively connected with the Focolare Movement; it is universal and can be lived by all."[7] From this "new spirituality" she envisions "men and women of almost every nation in the world today... trying to be, at least in their own area, seeds of a new people, for a world more united, a world of peace, giving special attention to the poor and powerless."[8]

Religious are intimately bound to this communitarian challenge; in fact, they are meant to lead the way. In *Vita consecrata*, John Paul II calls them to embrace this new spirituality with all their hearts.

John Paul II and Vita Consecrata

One of the most important themes of *Vita consecrata*, Pope John Paul II's post-synodal apostolic exhortation on the consecrated life, is that of "communion." This magisterial document provides a comprehensive and updated

---

4. Chiara Lubich, "A Spirituality of Communion," in *Essential Writings*, 27.

5. Chiara Lubich, "A New Way of Living," in *Essential Writings*, 14.

6. Ibid., 14; Idem, "Two Sides of the Same Coin," in *Essential Writings*, 19–26; Idem, "Jesus Forsaken," in *Essential Writings*, 88–97; Idem, "In the School of Jesus: Philosophy and Theology," in *Essential Writings*, 206; Idem, "Persons in Communion," in *Essential Writings*, 222–23; Idem, "The Dream of a God," in *Essential Writings*, 98–109.

7. Ibid., 15.

8. Ibid.

vision of both the nature and role of the consecrated life in the world today. It notes, "[C]onsecrated persons are asked to be true experts of communion and to practice the spirituality of communion as 'witnesses and architects of the plan for unity which is the crowning point of human history in God's design'" (*VC*, 46). According to John Paul II, the spirituality of communion is an interpretative key that unlocks the meaning of consecrated life and its significance for the Church and for the world in the post-Vatican II era. It is the theological and spiritual "hinge" upon which the rest of the document hangs, providing consecrated persons with a concrete way to unite theology and their day-to-day lives.

The Structure of Communion

Vita consecrata shows the centrality of the spirituality of communion for John Paul II, who clarifies his purpose at the outset: "Whereas the Second Vatican Council emphasized the profound reality of ecclesial communion, in which all gifts converge for the building up of the Body of Christ and for the Church's mission in the world, in recent years there has been felt the need to clarify *the specific identity of the various states of life*, their vocation and their particular mission in the Church" (*VC*, 4). This apostolic exhortation focuses precisely on the *specific identity* of the consecrated life. It encourages those who have dedicated their lives to following the evangelical counsels and provides them with "a deeper understanding of the great gift of the consecrated life in its three aspects of consecration, communion and mission" (*VC*, 13).

The exhortation's Trinitarian structure is especially suited to this aim. The *Introduction* describes the various forms of consecrated life as "a gift of God the Father to his Church through the Holy Spirit ... deeply rooted in the example and teaching of Christ the Lord" (*VC*, 1). At the *Conclusion* is a prayer to the Most Holy Trinity and an Invocation of the Blessed Virgin Mary (see *VC*, 11–12). Between those two points appear three interrelated chapters — *Confessio Trinitatis: The Origins of the Consecrated Life in the Mystery of Christ and of the Trinity*; *Signum Fraternitatis: Consecrated Life as a Sign of Communion in the Church*; and *Servitium Caritatis: Consecrated Life: Manifestation of God's Love in the World*. The Confession of the Trinity. A Sign of Fraternity. The Service of Charity. The exhortation follows a "high-descending" theology of the consecrated life. It roots the evangelical counsels in contemplation of the Transfigured Christ and, through him, in the very nature of the Godhead (see *VC*, 21). It presents the common life as "an eloquent sign of ecclesiastical communion" (*VC*, 42), discovering its mission in "the prophetic task of recalling and serving the divine plan for humanity" (*VC*, 73). The consecrated life, in other words, finds its *raison d'être* in Christ's revelation of the intimate relations of the Most Holy Trinity; its sign-value in its witness to the harmony of life in God, of which the Church as "a mystery of communion" is a concrete, visible sign; its mission not in external works alone, but "in making Christ present to the world through personal witness" (*VC*, 72). In this way, the consecrated life "indisputably belongs to the life and holiness of the Church" (*VC*, 29) and "expresses her very nature" (*VC*, 29). The document reinforces one central idea. "The idea of a Church made up only of sacred ministers and lay people does not … conform to the intentions of her divine Founder" (*VC*, 29). As John Paul II notes, quoting Teresa of Avila, " 'What would become of the world if there were no Religious?' " (*VC*, 105). "Without this concrete sign there would be a danger that the charity which animates the entire Church would grow cold, that the salvific paradox of the Gospel would be blunted, and that the 'salt' of faith would lose its savor in a world undergoing secularization" (*VC*, 105). In this light, the origins of the spirituality of communion become clear — Christ's intimate relations with the Father and the Holy Spirit. This fundamental concept of *communio* reveals the profound value of the consecrated life to the Church.

The Immediate Context

The phrase "spirituality of communion" first appears in the second chapter, "*Signum Fraternitatis*." The section entitled "*Sentire cum Ecclesia*" contains this passage:

A great task also belongs to the consecrated life in the light of the teaching about the Church as communion, so strongly proposed by the Second Vatican Council. Consecrated persons are asked to be true experts of communion and to practice the spirituality of communion as "witnesses and architects of the plan for unity which is the crowning point of human history in God's design." The sense of ecclesial communion, developing into a *spirituality of communion*, promotes a way of thinking, speaking and acting which enables the Church to grow in depth and extension. The life of communion in fact "becomes a *sign* for all the world and a compelling *force* that leads people to faith in Christ.... In this way communion leads to *mission*, and itself becomes mission"; indeed, "*communion begets communion*: in essence it is a *communion that is missionary*." (*VC*, 46)

As it continues, the document clarifies an important aspect of this spirituality of communion — "an allegiance of mind and heart to the Magisterium of the Bishops, an allegiance which must be lived honestly and clearly testified to before the People of God by all consecrated persons, especially those involved in theological research, teaching, publishing, catechesis and the use of the means of social communication" (*VC*, 46). To be sure, "because consecrated persons have a special place in the Church, their attitude in this regard is of immense importance for the whole People of God" (*VC*, 46). The document cites the testimonies of founders and foundresses who have demonstrated "a constant and lively sense of the Church" (*VC*, 46), figures such as Francis of Assisi, Catherine of Siena, Ignatius of Loyola, Teresa of Avila, and The Little Flower (*VC*, 46). These great saints, who maintained full ecclesial communion, exemplify for consecrated persons how "to resist the particularly strong centrifugal and disruptive forces at work today" (*VC*, 46). Speaking, thinking, and acting with the Magisterium, therefore, is one aspect of the vital missionary role consecrated persons have in the Church, continuing the venerable tradition of great saints, founders and foundresses, within a larger context of communion that itself begets communion. These ever-expanding contexts give an added richness to the concept of the spirituality of communion. Only by taking them into account can consecrated persons understand their important role in the post-Vatican II era and "be nourished *from the wellspring of a sound and deep spirituality*" (*VC*, 167).

Chapter Two contains another key text on the spirituality of communion. The subheading, "*Fraternity in a divided and unjust world*" notes that institutes of the consecrated life are given a specific task:

The Church entrusts to communities of consecrated life the particular task of *spreading the spirituality of communion*, first of all in their internal life and then in the ecclesial community, and even beyond its boundaries, by opening or continuing a dialogue in charity, especially where today's world is torn apart by ethnic hatred or senseless violence. Placed as they are within the world's different societies — societies frequently marked by conflicting passions and interests, seeking unity but uncertain about the ways to attain it — communities of consecrated life, where persons of different ages, languages and cultures meet as brothers and sisters, are *signs that dialogue is always possible* and that communion can bring differences into harmony. (*VC*, 51)

Earlier, this section expresses the hope "that all will grow in the understanding and spirituality of communion" (*VC*, 50). It also reiterates the obligation of fraternity as a form of witness to the Trinity: "By constantly promoting fraternal love, also in the form of the common life, the consecrated life has shown that *sharing in the Trinitarian communion can change human relationships* and create a new type of solidarity" (*VC*, 41), one in which everything is done "in communion and dialogue" (*VC*, 4) and favors a "'dialogue of life' which embodies a basic model of mission and of the proclamation of Christ's Gospel" (*VC*, 102). Consecrated persons are entrusted with three special tasks. They are to spread the spirituality of communion within themselves, within the ecclesial communion, and beyond its boundaries. Motivated by deep personal love for Christ (see *VC*, 84), they reach out in dialogue, "the new name of charity, especially charity within the Church" (*VC*, 74).

Consequences

What might this "particular task of *spreading the spirituality of communion*" (*VC*, 51) mean for members of institutes of consecrated life? The threefold framework of *internal life*, *ecclesial communion*, and *beyond* suggests the nature of this task.

Internal Life. Institutes of consecrated life must live in harmony: "In an age characterized by the globalization of problems and the return of the idols of nationalism, international Institutes especially are called to uphold and to bear witness to the sense of communion between peoples, races and cultures" (*VC*, 51). They do so by living out their common charism in communion with each other, even though they represent various age groups, nationalities, cultural backgrounds, and theological perspectives. Generating unity out of the diversity of their experience through dialogue demonstrates the communion of heart and mind to which all are called. Institutes of consecrated life should live out communion at every level — local, provincial, and general. In doing so, they should strive to maintain a spirit of cooperation among these various levels in keeping with the principle of subsidiarity.

Living the spirituality of communion within each particular community leads to cooperation among the different institutes (see *VC*, 52). Because they share a common call to the evangelical counsels, these institutes — both old and new — regard one another with respect and strive to work together to proclaim the Good News of Jesus Christ to the world. They maintain trusting, respectful concern for one another. The document recalls St. Bernard's words about the various religious orders:

> I admire them all. I belong to one of them by observance, but to all of them by charity. We all need one another: the spiritual good which I do not own and possess, I receive from others…. In this exile, the Church is still on pilgrimage and is, in a certain

sense, plural: she is a single plurality and a plural unity. All our diversities, which make manifest the richness of God's gifts, will continue to exist in the one house of the Father, which has many rooms. Now there is a division of graces; then there will be distinctions of glory. Unity, both here and there, consists in one and the same charity. (*VC*, 52)

In this spirit, the document encourages coordinating bodies such as the Conferences of Major Superiors and the Conferences of Secular Institutes to cooperate with each other, as well as with their particular country's episcopal conference. They are also encouraged "to maintain frequent and regular contacts with the Congregation for Institutes of Consecrated Life and Societies of Apostolic Life, as a sign of their communion with the Holy See" (*VC*, 53). A spirituality of communion lived within an institute of consecrated life itself should naturally overflow into relations beyond its boundaries.

Ecclesial Communion. The document also encourages relationships of mutual respect and collaboration between institutes of consecrated life and every level of ecclesial communion — other states of life within the Church (i.e., laity and clergy), as well as with brothers and sisters of the various Christian confessions. They should do this out of respect for the common dignity shared by all the faithful (*VC*, 31), but taking care that "the identity of the Institute in its internal life is not harmed" (*VC*, 56).

Cooperation with the laity receives special mention. The document notes that "many Institutes have concluded that *their charism can be shared with the laity*" (*VC*, 54). Such sharing takes many forms, from inviting others to live their spirituality to various kinds of pastoral collaboration. As a result, "the participation of the laity often brings unexpected and rich insights into certain aspects of the charism, leading to a more spiritual interpretation of it and helping to draw from it directions for new activities in the apostolate" (*VC*, 55). Emphasizing the equal dignity of men and women before God (*VC*, 57), the document touches on the specific role of consecrated women. It describes them as "signs of God's tender love towards the human race" (*VC*, 57) and points out that "women's new self-awareness also helps men to reconsider their way of looking at things, the way they understand themselves, where they place themselves in history and how they interpret it, and the way they organize social, political, economic, religious, and ecclesial life" (*VC*, 57).

Institutes of consecrated life also must give due attention to ecumenical dialogue. Such dialogue takes many forms — *lectio divina*, common prayer, friendship, hospitality, common undertakings of service, and witness. Promoting Christian unity is not just the work of institutes specifically founded for this purpose or that have discerned it later in their history: "[N]o Institute of Consecrated Life should feel itself dispensed from working for this cause" (*VC*, 101). The monastic tradition in the Eastern Catholic Churches is entrusted with promoting unity with the Orthodox Churches, and monasteries of contemplative life with "the spiritual ecumenism of prayer, conversion of heart, and charity" (*VC*, 101).

Beyond. The spirituality of communion moves consecrated persons beyond the Christian communion into dialogue with other faiths and cultures: "Because 'inter-religious dialogue is a part of the Church's evangelizing mission,' Institutes of Consecrated Life cannot exempt themselves from involvement also in this field, each in accordance with its own charism and following the directives of ecclesiastical authority" (*VC*, 102). They do this primarily through "the testimony of a life of poverty, humility and chastity, imbued with fraternal love for all" (*VC*, 102). Dedicated to proclaiming the Good News through a "dialogue of life," they "promote appropriate forms of exchange, marked by cordial friendship and mutual sincerity, with monastic communities of other religions" (*VC*, 102). Other areas for cooperation at this level include promoting the sanctity of human life and the dignity of women (*VC*, 102). All such efforts require proper formation, and study and research, together with deep faith and personal and spiritual maturity (*VC*, 102).

Finally, institutes of consecrated life place themselves at the service of all humanity through "a life of self-giving love" (*VC*, 75). Indeed, "the fact that consecrated persons fix their gaze on the Lord's countenance does not diminish their commitment on behalf of humanity; on the contrary, it strengthens this commitment, enabling it to have an impact on history, in order to free history from all that disfigures it" (*VC*, 75). First and foremost, consecrated men and women offer "the witness of a life given totally to God and to their brothers and sisters, in imitation of the Saviour who, out of love for humanity, made himself a servant" (*VC*, 76). They live a life of genuine inculturation, one that "requires attitudes similar to those of the Lord when he became man and walked among us in love and meekness" (*VC*, 79). In their service as "a Gospel leaven within a culture, purifying and perfecting it" (*VC*, 80), they follow the Church in its preferential option for those "*in situations of greater weakness*" (*VC*, 82), particularly "the poor, in varied states of affliction…those on the margins of society, the elderly, the sick, the young, any and all who are considered and treated as 'the least' " (*VC*, 82).

Specifically, they meet the needs of the poor through medical care, education, social communications, and the evangelization of culture (see *VC*, 83, 96–99). Their life of evangelical poverty, moreover, *"is a value in itself"* which, "accompanied by a preferential love for the poor" is expressed "especially by sharing the conditions of life of the most neglected" (*VC*, 90). "[M]any communities … live and work among the poor and the marginalized; they embrace their conditions of life and share in their sufferings, problems and perils" (*VC*, 90).

The spirituality of communion, kindled by God in institutes of consecrated life, spreads throughout the Church. Arising within a particular institute where members of various ages, cultures, and educational backgrounds live together in a spirit of fraternal love, it reaches out to other institutes, to other states of life within the Church, to other Christian denominations, to other religions, and to all of humanity. It does so in a spirit of dialogue and service that witnesses to the personal presence of Christ in the world and to the power of the Trinity to transform human relationships. This spirituality builds relationships of solidarity wherever human beings congregate, a sign of the intimate life with God to which all are called.

Observations

John Paul II's description of the spirituality of communion resembles a series of concentric circles that begin with God and radiate out to the institutes of consecrated life, to various levels of ecclesial communion, and to relationships of dialogue and collaboration beyond. With certain adaptations, this spirituality can be lived out in other states of life within the Church (i.e., both clerical and lay) as a way of giving witness to the mystery of Church as *communio*. The spirituality of communion thus forms part of the common spiritual treasury of all believers in the saving mystery of Christ. It is fundamental to the lives of *all* believers, particularly to consecrated men and women, who live out a spirituality of communion through the evangelical counsels and the common life.

In the light of the spirituality of communion, the counsels must be considered "above all a gift of the Holy Trinity" (*VC*, 20). They "*make visible* the marvels wrought by God in the frail humanity of those who are called" (*VC*, 20), rendering consecrated life "one of the tangible seals which the Trinity impresses upon history, so that people can sense with longing the attraction of the divine beauty" (*VC*, 20). This is so because the counsels express the fundamental Christological and Trinitarian dimensions — "the love of the Son for the Father in the unity of the Holy Spirit" (*VC*, 21). Christ and the Trinity, in other words, are the practitioners *par excellence* of the spirituality of communion; through vows, consecrated persons participate in that life which one day they wish to behold fully.

In the context of a spirituality of communion, the vow of chastity manifests *"dedication to God with an undivided heart"* and reflects *"the infinite love which links the three Divine Persons in the mysterious depths of the life of the Trinity"* (*VC*, 21). Chastity is a visible sign of the coming kingdom and a constant reminder of God's solidarity with the human race. Despite the limitation of the imperfect human beings who try to live chastity, it proclaims that "*the power of God's love can accomplish great things* precisely within the context of human love" (*VC*, 88). As with all the counsels, chastity reminds others of their call to holiness, particularly as a sign of hope in the transforming power of God's love to bring about the kingdom that is to come. The vow of chastity points beyond the limitations of the present world to "the pure love which consecrated persons draw from the contemplation of Trinitarian love, revealed to us in Christ" (*VC*, 88).

Poverty "proclaims that God is man's only real treasure," becoming "an expression of that total gift of self which the three Divine Persons make to one another*" (VC, 21)*. It challenges *"materialism which craves possessions"* (*VC*, 89), offers itself in service of the poor, and attests "that God is the true wealth of the human heart" (*VC*, 90). Although there are many ways to live it, evangelical poverty expresses itself in a witness "accompanied by a preferential love for the poor" (*VC*, 90). The vow of poverty is a reminder of God's special love for the poor and marginalized. Like Christ, consecrated persons seek only the love of God. The spirit of poverty frees them to "give themselves without reserve in the service of the most disadvantaged people on earth" and to "promote projects of solidarity for the benefit of the poor" (*VC*, 89).

The vow of obedience manifests "the liberating beauty of a dependence which is not servile but filial … a reflection in history of the loving harmony between the three Divine Persons" (VC, 21). It challenges "those *notions of freedom* which separate this fundamental human good from its essential relationship to the truth and to moral norms" (*VC*, 91). Through their lives, consecrated persons proclaim that *"there is no contradiction between obedience and freedom"* and, like Christ, they disclose "the mystery of obedience as the path of obedience to the Father's will, and the mystery of obedience as the path to the gradual conquest of true freedom" (*VC*, 91). Such human obedience is rooted in Christ's obedience to the will of the Father and, for consecrated persons, manifests itself in filial love of the teachings and directives of the Church and of the expressed desires of their legitimate superiors. Such obedience presumes a spirit of open dialogue and intense listening.

The common life provides a concrete sign in the world that proclaims: "the Father, who desires to make all of humanity one family...the Incarnate Son, who gathers the redeemed into unity ... and the Holy Spirit as the principle of unity in the Church" (*VC*, 21). This communal dimension of the consecrated life is "the particular sign, before the Church and society of the bond which comes from the same call and the common desire ... to be obedient to that call" (*VC*, 92). It proclaims the power of God to transform all human relationships (no matter how tangled or distorted) and to those who partake of it offers a foretaste of the Kingdom to come. Life in community becomes the laboratory or workshop in which the spirituality of communion is forged, tested, and gradually perfected in the course of daily living. Common life provides the environment in which the intimate relations of the Trinity become transposed to the lives of consecrated persons. Through them, those inside and outside the boundaries of the ecclesial communion are strengthened with the very life of the Trinity.

For religious, the spirituality of communion should spark a renewed appreciation of their original charism. Vatican II called for a sensitive renewal of religious life that began with "the constant return to the sources of Christian life in general, and the original genius of religious foundations in particular; together with the modifications of such foundations to accommodate new circumstances" (*PC*, 2). John Paul II rightly points out the importance of the vision of founders and foundresses, and of the spiritualities that inspired them (*VC*, 46). These spiritualities work together with the deep gospel inspiration of the spirituality of communion to renew the charism of the various institutes and bring about deep transformation in their members. Chiara Lubich puts it this way: "So that religious orders may shine with the true spirituality for which they were born and have their reason for existence, their followers must see their founders as God sees them. God sees in St. Francis the idea of poverty, which in God is love; in St. Thérèse the idea of 'the little way' which in God is love; in St. Catherine the blood of Christ which in God is Love."[9] In this light, the various charisms and spiritualities that inspired religious orders and their founders maintain their unique insights into God's providential plan for humanity, yet are one in living the gospel.

Finally, through the spirituality of communion religious appreciate more and more deeply the "communion of saints." John Paul II points out the "tremendous need for saints" (*VC*, 35) and the meaning of the universal call to holiness for religious: "The fact that all are called to be saints cannot fail to inspire more and more those who by their very choice of life have the mission of reminding others of that call" (*VC*, 39). He points to the great saints and founders: "These testimonies are representative of the full ecclesial communion which the Saints, founders and foundresses, who lived in full ecclesial communion with the Church even "in diverse and often difficult times and circumstances" (*VC*, 46) and who preserved the prophetic dimension of consecrated life, turning it into a "Gospel leaven" by immersing themselves in their world without being overcome by it (*VC*, 80). He calls for "strong personalities inspired by saintly fervor" (*VC*, 81) and issues religious this challenge: "Dare to become part of the great movements of holiness which renowned saints have launched in their following of Christ" (*VC*, 106). He reminds them of the many saints throughout the Church's history who have devoted themselves to God through the consecrated life and have accomplished so much good (*VC*, 108). What the spirituality of communion and the communion of saints

---

9. Chiara Lubich, "Church as Communion," in *Essential Writings*, 114.

share is God's divinizing power, which transforms lives and enables human beings to share in the fellowship of Christ's disciples and the intimate life of the Trinity. Chiara Lubich describes this unity of the communion of saints: "The lives of the saints are identical even though they vary greatly. Once they have given themselves to God, he takes them under his special care, and as supreme artist and supreme Love, he makes them into divine masterpieces."[10] Living as a saint and dying as a saint goes to the heart of the Jesus' call to gospel fellowship, a call that consecrated men and women have heeded.

Conclusion

The spirituality of communion is essential for religious life. John Paul II saw the possibility of an "actual breakdown of the consecrated life, a collapse which is not measured by a decrease in numbers but by a failure to cling steadfastly to the Lord and to personal vocation and mission" (*VC*, 63). He proposes a spirituality of communion as the means by which consecrated persons can avoid such a crisis. It permeates his apostolic exhortation, *Vita consecrata*; it provides an interpretative key for understanding the consecrated life. Through the spirituality of communion, consecrated persons fulfill their mission of clinging steadfastly to the Lord and remind others of the universal call to holiness, a call to participate in Christ's transfigured, glorified body.

Communion begets communion, and is fundamentally missionary in nature (*VC*, 46). Because "the sense of mission is at the very heart of every form of consecrated life" (*VC*, 25), religious, as faithful practitioners of a spirituality of communion, point beyond themselves to the intimate relations of the Trinity, striving in all they do to establish

---

10. Ibid., 115.

similar bonds of solidarity with people all over the world. The anthropological basis of the spirituality of communion flows from the very nature of the Godhead: God creates and sustains humanity; humanity exists and acts as *imago Dei*. In this sense, what John Paul II says to religious aptly summarizes the spirituality of communion: "Make your lives a fervent expectation of Christ; go forth to meet him like the wise virgins setting out to meet the Bridegroom. Be always ready, faithful to Christ, the Church, to your Institute and to the men and women of our time. In this way you will day by day be renewed in Christ, in order with his Spirit to build fraternal communities, to join him in washing the feet of the poor, and to contribute in your own unique way to the transfiguration of the world" (*VC*, 110).

Living out such a vision of the consecrated life may seem difficult (if not impossible) in a confused and fragmented world. The next chapter proposes how religious can maintain values within their communities through tested, life-giving, virtue-bearing structures.

Reflection Questions

What are the unique challenges of living the spirituality of communion?

Which of these do you find most difficult? Are there any that you find easier (or more difficult) than others? In what sense does "communion beget communion"? In what sense is the experience of communion also missionary in nature? Why must the dialogue of communion begin from within and work itself outwards? Is it possible to be in communion with members of other faith communities and not your own? Is it possible to be in communion with strangers and not with those closest to you? What steps can you take to encourage living a spirituality of communion in your own religious community?

5

Virtue and Community Structures

When people join a community they must realize that they are coming from this environment of sin and that everyone's heart harbors the evils which corrode communion. Ours are communities of sinners, just as the Church is holy but composed of sinners. It is clear, then, that to arrive at *koinonia* it is necessary to pass through *metanonia*.

Fabio Ciardi, *Koinonia*[1]

When communities require conversion, as the words above suggest, a "spirituality of communion" can provide concrete ways of facilitating it. This holds true especially in the area of virtue. In order to thrive, religious communities need to foster a deep-seated appreciation of the excellence of a life of virtue. An increasing number of religious, however, have difficulty seeing how traditional structures of religious life can help them preserve and nourish their vocations and face daunting institutional uncertainties with confidence. The value of structures has come into question not because they lack verve or

---

1. Ciardi, *Koinonia*, 324.

purpose, but because of something deeper. Since the end of Vatican II, the culture of religious life in the Catholic Church has changed substantially. Its institutions — once vibrant centers of life and vigor — have lost sight of the importance of mediating the life of the virtues to their members. By overlooking such a basic area of concern, many of these structures have grown stale and no longer inspire the people they claim to serve.

Caught Off Guard

Have the institutional structures ever succeeded in instilling a deep love for the virtuous life? Nostalgia may exaggerate the accomplishments of a particular religious institution and its structures. On the other hand, it is important to acknowledge that most of the structures of religious life were established precisely to help members of the community grow in the practice of the virtues. The Benedictines stress *laus perennis* ("perennial praise"); the Jesuits require performing the spiritual exercises; the Redemptorists meditate on the monthly virtues — to name but a few. The truth probably lies somewhere between pessimism and optimism. Although mistakes — sometimes grave ones — were made in the past, more often than not the structures did achieve the general purposes for which they were created.

"Success," however, "is the unwary harbinger of decline." If a few key operating assumptions are changed, formulas for growth that worked — sometimes for centuries — unexpectedly come up short. The sweeping changes following the Second Vatican Council caught many traditional religious communities off guard. Rather than adapting their institutional structures to the needs and challenges of the world around them, these communities presumed that past formulas for success would carry them through troubled times. In doing so, the future passed them by, without them realizing what had happened. Many found themselves caught in a whirlwind of unfocused apathy and discontent with little insight into just what went wrong or how to make things right. Frustrated by structures that no longer seemed capable of responding to the needs of their members, some overreacted by discarding their formulas without putting anything in their place.

In Defense of Structures

This discussion assumes that a religious community possesses virtue in common and that it is acquired, at least in part, when its members remain faithful to the structures that best express its charism. "Virtue" may be defined, on its most basic level, as a habit of the soul that enables a person to see, judge, and act with common sense. "Structure," in turn, signifies any officially required common action or communal framework in a religious community. Virtue and structure are related. A person becomes virtuous not through his or her own efforts, but through a web of interlocking personal, social, and divine influences. Through structures, religious communities pass on their values from one generation to the next.

Structures help to nurture virtues in the life of the individual. The virtues dispose a person to act in accordance with reason — understood not as a mere minimalist sense of tightly controlled syllogisms and univocal logic, but as a broad openness to reality. Reason allows for appropriate correlations between individual and corporate action (e.g., the philosophical distinction between microcosm and macrocosm). When consistently followed, structures established for reasonable ends can assist a person in pursuing a life of virtue. Adherence to reasonably ordered structures will contribute to the formation of good dispositions in community members. The stability of religious life rests on the formidable task of discerning those structures which best serve to build the community by forming individuals.

Religious communities face troubles if they do not appreciate sufficiently the usefulness of structure in individuals' moral and spiritual lives. Sound structures can instill values and help religious along the way of perfection; without them, a community will be weakened by subtle relativism and implicit individualism. Structure can assist religious to live a life of virtue; when it is missing or irrelevant, individuals fall back on their own resources and "go it alone." The results can be devastating: the vows can become mere abstractions with little bearing on daily life; community members share little (if any) of their lives with one another; common life devolves into mere physical presence or a convenient "bed and breakfast" arrangement.

What to Do

How can the culture of religious life change? How can virtues be integrated into institutional structures? What criteria determine the values to be promoted by the structures of religious communities? A number of suggestions come to mind.

Using structures to nurture virtue in the lives of community members does not mean simply reinstating the structures in place before all the changes. The contemporary Western world view that permeates much of religious life cannot be avoided, escaped, or ignored. Structures from the past are not necessarily useful in addressing current challenges.

*This is so because the structures of a religious commu-
nity have both internal and external points of focus. The
internal has to do with the organization of community life
and the spiritual welfare of the members; the external,
with the witness value this structure has for the world at
large.* Each is intricately related to the other. Members
lose confidence if they no longer believe that their internal community structures have intrinsic value for the
world at large — and vice versa. Community structures
— even countercultural ones related to the counsels and
the common life — must be in dialogue with the world.
When they do not, structures become a kind of communal escapism.

*Converting the structures of a religious community
requires realistic assessment of those already in place.*
Members must ascertain how structures first developed
and whether they are meeting the needs of the present
community. To do so, the community must examine the
original purpose for these structures and ask themselves if
they truly serve the community's present corporate project. Other structural options that meet the same needs
can be examined and evaluated to determine whether
they truly encourage virtuous living. By scrutinizing their
structures of community living, members can come to
recognize the ways of relating to one another that help or
harm the day-to-day running of their institutions.

*Religious life depends upon a healthy rapport between
the individual and the community.* When evaluating
existing structures or when attempting to implement new
ones, members must take care to set for themselves a middle course between the extremes of rugged individualism
and institutional uniformity. Structures can and should
be developed to concentrate precisely on this point. A

healthy, functional relationship between the individual and the institution begins early in the formation process, when members learn to integrate their personal lives with their community's corporate existence.

Implementing new structures as a means of encouraging the virtues should be built on existing traditions. New structures need not replicate those used in earlier, more prosperous circumstances. Doing so might have the opposite effect of encouraging subtle forms of self-deception and escapism. Every effort should be made, however, to insure a certain degree of continuity between a community's established traditions and the new structures it may choose to implement for the good of its members.

Start small. The culture of religious communities declines slowly, mainly through indifference and neglect. Implementing a few well-chosen initiatives and building on their anticipated success will probably reap better results than many innovations in a short time. People need time to adapt to a change in structure. Concentrated yet limited enthusiasm can generate some change; fundamental improvement requires persistent and patient planning.

Structures should not be implemented without the support of the majority of the community, but leaders should not hold back on account of a vocal minority. All points of view must be given due respect; once made, however, a decision should be implemented without delay. Proposed changes should be explained to those who disagree and attempts should be made to demonstrate their worth. These proposals should not be watered down, however, to satisfy the complaints of a few. Sometimes exceptions are needed, but everyone should be integrated as soon as possible into the mainstream of community life.

To emphasize the purpose for the changes, a process should be implemented by which community members can interpret reasons for making them, and highlight the relationship between the new structures and the life of the virtues. However this is done — in community meetings, review of life, study sessions — the primary concern should be to link the structural functioning of the community and how the proposed changes help to instill the life of the virtues. Through such a process, the community would concentrate first on the meaning of virtue and its various enumerations (theological, cardinal, and so forth), then on the types of structure common in religious communities (hierarchical, collaborative, therapeutic), and finally concentrate on studying in detail the relationship between the two.

Structures should help people build relationships based on understanding and trust. Sound friendships are essential to fostering the virtuous life. These should be actively encouraged in religious life, primarily among the members themselves, but also with those outside the community. Although some suspect that friendships among members can threaten the community's corporate identity, such relationships should be understood as treasures that inspire the life of the virtues. Members should discern the different types of friendship (utilitarian, pleasure, character) and be encouraged to nurture relationships that will lead them and their community along the way of virtue.

The ideal of living a life of virtue should be reinforced in the religious community. Periodic evaluations can determine whether the structures in place are achieving their intended purposes. Every religious community has the same primary goal — to bring its members and the people they serve into an ever deeper union with God.

The virtues keep this goal in focus and provide the means of achieving it. A vital community never stops revisiting and renewing its purpose and the means for achieving it.

These suggestions represent but a few of the concrete steps that can be taken to form structures of community living and to help members progress in the life of virtue. They assume that, when properly planned and scrutinized, structures can help religious to achieve their deepest hopes of living in harmony with one another, with those they serve, and with the God they love.

Structures, Conversion, and Grace

Even useful structures, however, have inherent limits. Despite their value in facilitating a reasoned life, in and of themselves, they cannot carry religious to the threshold of divine love. Human efforts alone cannot make people convert. Spiritual transformation — personal as well as social — comes about mainly through the initiative of divine grace and only secondarily through human response. Even the latter depends on God's providential care. For this reason, religious must take care to keep structure in proper perspective. Overstructuring the community's environment might relegate God's grace to its periphery of concerns and cause it to rely on pre-established formulas. Over-reliance on structures, in other words, can shut out the quiet movement of the Spirit. To offset this dangerous tendency, community structures must be open and flexible enough to allow the Spirit to enter among community members and to make the divine presence felt in their hearts. Inflexible structures risk stifling the voice of God in their lives. A religious community exists not to perpetuate itself, but to make God present among the members, and among the people it serves.

A Look to the Sacraments

The structures of community living work in a fashion analogous to the Church's sacraments. The seven sacraments are divine structures or institutions — "outward signs *instituted* by Christ to give grace." Although the sacramental life of the Church has changed over its history, that which makes each of them part and parcel of the supernatural life of Christ's Mystical Body remains constant. These external structures, which mediate the internal grace of divine life to those who receive them, cannot exist apart from the sacrament of Christ, which is the Church. Nor can the Church exist apart from the sacrament of God, who is Jesus Christ. The Church's sacramental life has a single purpose — to enable the love of God to permeate the life of its members and to vivify their daily activities. Sacramental graces, then, flow into the structures of community life.

The sacraments, in other words, provide a template for organizing the structures of community living. Among other things, this implies that community structures should consist of both word and sign, be rooted in the Scriptures, inspire both the mind and heart of the community, focus on the community's journey to God in faith, deal with the life cycle of community members from birth to death, address the reality of failure in their individual lives and in the community as a whole, be open to change and adaptation, and emphasize both the end of human existence (union with God) and the means of attaining that end (a life of virtue). Community structures that correspond with these elements will be closely bonded to the Church, and through the Church to Christ.

How can the structures of religious life reinforce their members' faith? How can members be confident in the structures that express their corporate identity? If structures no longer correspond to the needs of a community's members and the people they serve, how can those structures be transformed? Deep-seated problems have no easy solutions, but it is certainly true that a community which does not humbly submit its structures to the transforming power of God's grace has little hope of surviving. Such submission to the divine comes only through the practiced discipline of prayer and a process of ongoing theological reflection dedicated to making concrete structural changes that correspond to the community's charism. Only by such efforts can a religious community, whatever its age or reputation, engage in constant conversion from "this environment of sin."

Conclusion

The future of religious life depends not so much on those who have publicly professed the evangelical counsels, but on the One to whom they entrust their lives and on whom they depend for their salvation. Religious communities cannot grow and thrive on their own. By being rooted deeply in the Spirit of God, they will live to serve future generations according to the charism for which they were founded. Those experiencing a "crisis" in their religious life need to root themselves again and trust in the Spirit.

"Spirit" and "structure" are not opposites. The two stand at odds with one another from time to time, but a close examination of the history of religious life shows that more often than not, structure and Spirit have worked together to do great things for the Church and the world it serves. To live a life according to the Spirit is to live a life of virtue, a life of reason, a life fully human.

More than anything else, religious communities need to develop closer contact with their own humanity. They need to integrate every dimension of their lives — the bodily, emotional, intellectual, spiritual, and social — and show who they are as individuals bound together in communal life and what they are called to become in the eyes of God. The structures of community life *can* be organized so that these dimensions, individually and together, work for the good of the community members and the people they serve. They can be reorganized, however, only by those willing to embrace *conversio*. Communion, as mentioned at the beginning of this chapter, requires conversion. True conversion, as the next chapter demonstrates, depends upon seeking out and accepting the grace-filled power to persevere.

Reflection Questions

Besides poverty, chastity, and obedience, what other virtues are important for life in a religious community? Why are they so important? What values do they underscore? How can they be encouraged? Which kinds of structures promote them (e.g., meditation in common, visits to the Blessed Sacrament, review of life)? Which of the virtues vital for the life of the community are particularly important for your religious community? What makes your community distinctive? Which virtues or values are distinctive in it? Which specific structures might your community adopt that could highlight this distinctiveness?

6
The Courage to Persist

You have not only a glorious history to remember and to recount, but also *a great history still to be accomplished!* Look to the future, where the Spirit is sending you in order to do even greater things.

John Paul II, *Vita consecrata*[1]

"So let us not grow weary of doing what is right, for we will reap at harvest time, if we do not give up" (Gal 6:9). These words of St. Paul highlight the importance of following Christ to the end, even in trying and difficult times. Doing so constitutes the virtue of perseverance — "to persist long in some undertaking until it is accomplished."[2] All Christians are called to persevere in their vocations. The vocation of the religious consists in Christian discipleship lived in a community dedicated to the evangelical counsels of chastity, poverty, and obedience. This is their one, consuming lifetime project.

Perseverance, for religious, is both personal and communal. They persevere as individuals by remaining

---

1. John Paul II, *Vita consecrata*, no. 110.
2. Thomas Aquinas, *Summa theologiae*, II–II q. 137, a. 1, resp. [The English quotation comes from the Blackfriars edition].

faithful to their vows and to their community until death. They persevere as a community by being conscientious in implementing their institute's charism and mission. This chapter will explore the many facets of perseverance and make specific observations about its special relevance for religious, offering practical suggestions for persevering in their vocation in their daily lives.

Perseverance as a Virtue

Traditionally, theologians connect perseverance to the cardinal virtue of fortitude, which moderates the passions of fear and daring in the face of great evils, especially in connection with the dangers of death. Perseverance is demonstrated by individuals who withstand difficulties, particularly those that arise from some delay in pursuing a lifelong task.[3] It is closely associated with patience, constancy, and hope. "To persist long in some undertaking until it is accomplished," a person must endure the sufferings of the present moment (patience), for an extended period of time (constancy) with expectation of achieving a future goal (hope). Marathon runners, for example, persevere by taking one step at a time, over and over again, to reach the finish line. They finish the race by performing every single step as well as they can. In a similar way, the disciple of Christ is called to run the good race all the way to the end. St. Paul uses a similar metaphor from sports: "Athletes deny themselves all sorts of things. They do this to win a crown of leaves that withers, but we a crown that is imperishable" (1 Cor 9:25). And again: "I do not run like a man who loses sight of the finish line. I do not fight as if I were shadowboxing. What I do is discipline my own

---

3. The presentation of perseverance in this section comes primarily from Thomas Aquinas, *Summa theologiae*, II–II, qq. 137–38.

body and master it, for fear that after having preached to others I myself would be rejected" (1 Cor 9:26–27).

By themselves, however, Christians cannot progress along the path of discipleship. Following Christ entails living in community, listening to his Word, and being led by his Spirit together. Although each individual must do his or her part, they do so as part of a complex nexus of factors. Perseverance in Christian discipleship requires discipline and training of the whole person (body, soul, and spirit) through such tried and true means as receiving the sacraments, prayer, fasting, penance, and almsgiving. It also requires the continuous support of divine grace. No one can persist in his or her vocation without the help of God. Such help comes either directly through the movement of God's Spirit in individuals' hearts or indirectly through the words and actions of other people. Although at times the act of persevering may seem solitary, it can only be done in community.

As a virtue, perseverance requires moderation. Closely tied to fortitude, it seeks to educate the irascible passions in order to develop the endurance to maintain the long struggle for a worthwhile goal. In its search for a middle way, perseverance tries to avoid the exaggerated extremes of "softness" and "obstinacy." The former concerns the tendency to give up a particular pursuit after encountering resistance. The "soft" do not seek the proper help and the required training for the inevitable obstacles they will encounter in the pursuit of a specific goal. In terms of Christian discipleship, they have not allowed the Good News to take root in the soil of the soul. As a result, at the slightest difficulty they lose heart (see Mk 4:1–9). The "obstinate," in contrast, tend to persist in a certain way even after it clearly is the wrong direction. They refuse to change their course of action even after reason itself has revealed the need for such a change. They have taken a wrong turn in the pursuit of a particular goal, yet resist admitting the mistake. For a Christian, being headstrong in mind and heart prevents the Spirit from working. Their refusal to adapt to new information and changing circumstances hinders them from heeding the Spirit in order to follow Christ in a truly liberating and selfless way.

Perseverance in Religious Life

Religious life has been likened to martyrdom. When the age of persecution ended in the early Church, the zeal to give oneself over completely to Christ found an outlet in Christian monasticism. Rather than dying for Christ literally, the early monks died to the world through lives dedicated to the evangelical counsels and a daily regimen of ascetical practices (e.g., prayer, fasting, manual labor).[4] Although religious life has changed since those desert fathers, today's religious are the spiritual heirs of this early, powerful movement of Christian asceticism.

Martyrdom, both old and new, is considered the principal act of the virtue of fortitude.[5] Although the possibility of martyrdom still exists in many parts of the world, most religious demonstrate the courage to give their lives for Christ through perseverance in their vocations. It is unlikely that they will be asked to die for Christ in a single decisive moment through violent means, so they give their lives through lifelong dedication to discipleship, patterning their lives on the way Jesus lived when he walked this earth. By forming community and following in the footsteps of the poor, obedient, and chaste Christ, they present a countercultural challenge to the world around them as well

---

4. See Claude J. Peifer, *Monastic Spirituality* (New York: Sheed and Ward, 1966), 185–86.

5. See Thomas Aquinas, *Summa theologiae*, II–II, q. 124, aa. 2–3.

as an eschatological sign of the coming of the kingdom. Perseverance is essential for life in community and for the vows. It strengthens religious to avoid the extremes of softness or obstinacy in their witness to the world.

Chastity. Religious persevere in chastity by recognizing their sexual feelings so that they can sublimate them in appropriate and constructive ways. They do so by acknowledging their sexuality (attractions, difficulties) and developing healthy friendships with members of both sexes. Doubts about chastity usually revolve around questions of intimacy. Like every human being, religious need to demonstrate loving attention and to disclose themselves in intimate relationships.[6] Doing so requires establishing and maintaining deep friendships without compromising their promises to the Lord. Religious, then, need to determine boundaries within such close relationships; crossing such boundaries sends a warning signal to set the friendship back on a proper course. They should have access to psychological testing, counseling, and spiritual direction to help them integrate their vow of chastity into a coherent, balanced life.

Poverty. In following Christ, religious need to examine the internal and external dimensions of their life of poverty. The call to be "poor in spirit" (Mt 5:3) gives Christ's disciples a simplicity that frees them from attachment to persons, places, and things. From this simplicity of heart, the true witness of poverty flows. To persevere in their vow of poverty, religious need to keep before themselves how their lifestyle conveys their witness to the gospel. They also need to reflect often on how they are applying their rule of life, even in small decisions and actions.

6. See Pat Collins, *Intimacy and the Hungers of the Heart* (Dublin/Mystic, Conn.: The Columba Press/Twenty-Third Publications, 1991), 142.

Perseverance in poverty is directly related to choices that both the community and its individual members make about food, clothing, furniture, and, most of all, the possession and use of money. While religious are not called to live in destitution, their lifestyles should be simple, uncluttered, and roughly equivalent from one community of the same institute to the next. Perseverance moderates whatever anxiety religious might feel because they have less, and it challenges those within the community who tend toward extremes — be it luxury or penury.

Obedience. Religious can model their perseverance in the vow of obedience on Jesus' openness to the will of his Father, an obedience that flowed from a deep, intimate relationship rooted in love, respect, and mutual dialogue. Such perseverance means being ready and willing to serve the community or the people of God, even without fully understanding why a particular service is asked of them. Obedience can never require something that contradicts a person's conscience, but much can be requested within areas that do not compromise moral judgment. Obedience is neither "soft" nor "obstinate." Softness bends the rules and interprets the clear will of a superior so that it corresponds to an individual's own designs. Obstinacy recognizes the rules of the community and the will of a superior, but refuses to obey out of stubbornness. Perseverance in obedience will take root in a particular community if its members (especially superiors) practice the art of dialogue and the understanding, empathy, and challenge that accompany it.

Community. Persevering in community life requires realistic strategies for balancing individual needs with group responsibilities. Such strategies must focus on concrete issues like presence in community, decision-making, community prayer, and sharing — to name but a few. Community dynamics depend, to a great extent, on the individual members. No two communities are alike, even those within the same religious institute. For this reason, members on the provincial and local levels need to adapt the general practices promoted by the institute to their local needs. In making such adaptations, the local community should focus on the common good, while taking into account its members' particular needs. Once again, persevering requires following a middle way. "Softness" in community life can be either personal or communal. An individual member may choose to opt out of community life rather than facing up to the inevitable difficulties. An entire community can become "soft" if the responsibilities normally required of community life are lowered to a bare minimum. "Obstinacy" can also be either personal or communal. Individuals may refuse to adapt to a community's rule of life simply because they do not coincide with their personal opinions. In like manner, an entire community may resist examining its lifestyle or way of living because they fear change.

Through perseverance, religious face the daily obstacles of life and endure in their vocations until the very end. As a virtue, it steers a middle course and has concrete relevance for communal and personal dedication to the evangelical counsels.

Observations

Emphasis on the virtue of perseverance can help religious to face problems large and small with even stronger resolve. Communities can rediscover this important element of their heritage through seven concrete actions.

Self-Reflection. Religious should not only persevere, but also grow in the spiritual life. Self-knowledge is an important foundation for such growth. To follow Christ to the end, they should identify their strengths and weaknesses. By doing so they will understand where growth should take place and how they should go about accomplishing it. Practical helps such as the examination of conscience and review of life can be particularly helpful in this regard. Spiritual direction and conversations with close friends can also help religious persevere and grow.

Petitionary Prayer. Persevering requires God's help, help that is readily available. Anyone can receive God's bountiful grace simply by asking for it. By humbly praying for the grace of perseverance, individually and as a community, religious will receive the help they need — and more. They should be fearless about identifying their needs and bringing them to God. They can open their hearts and ask God for the courage and strength to live out their vocations until the very end.

Daily Formational Practices. To persevere, religious must cooperate with the graces they ask for and have received. They can do so through daily practices that train their hearts and minds to face inevitable obstacles. Such practices might include traditional sacramental and ascetical means (prayer, spiritual reading, the liturgy, acts of charity, and so forth) or any innovations they find helpful. However they go about it, it is important that religious consciously use such practices to bolster their individual and communal lives. These practices are not an end in themselves, but a means to continuing growth in the religious life.

Genuine Friendships. To grow and persevere in their vocations, religious need intimate friendships. Such relationships should be oriented toward the good (becoming virtuous) and particularly oriented toward life in community and the evangelical counsels. These friendships should be open to others. They should also display the typical marks of friendship, such as benevolence, reciprocity, and mutual indwelling.[7] Close friends offer a sounding board against which hopes and disappointments can be expressed in a safe, trusting environment. With them, it is easier to face life's obstacles. By establishing and cultivating such friendships, religious maintain an essential openness to themselves, to others, and to God.

Community Activities. Religious grow and persevere in their vocations through community. Community activities, expressed in the structures and means of relating to one another, contribute to the members' overall good. To make best use of activities such as common prayer, meals, study, and recreation, they need to reflect on their way of life and identify how they can live it even better. The criteria for such self-evaluation should include the witness value of their lifestyle and the manner in which issues relating to individual freedom and communal responsibility are resolved. Requirements for community activities should avoid the extremes of softness (laxness) and obstinacy (rigidity).

Relations beyond Community. For religious to grow and persevere in their vocations, communities and their individual members need to foster healthy relationships beyond their particular setting. These relationships include those in the various levels of their own institute (local, provincial, general), as well as in parishes, denominational churches, associations, clubs, or other

---

7. See Thomas Aquinas, *Summa* theologiae, II–II, q. 23, a. 1, resp. For a development of these characteristics, see Paul J. Wadell, *Friendship and the Moral Life* (Notre Dame, Ind.: University of Notre Dame Press, 1989), 130–41.

organizations. While maintaining their countercultural and eschatological witness to the world, religious can present to the community at large their interest in and concern for the welfare of all. Although the character of these extra-community relations will vary from one place to another — depending, for example, whether a community is contemplative or active — they should be marked by a spirit of hospitality and welcome. Hospitality fosters perseverance and growth — and vice versa. To grow and thrive, a community must open itself to its neighbors.

Charism and Mission. Finally, to grow and persevere in their vocations religious need to dedicate themselves to the charism and mission of their own institute. From the very beginning, candidates for religious life need to learn about the theories and practices of the work to which they will be dedicating their lives. They should be encouraged, moreover, to allow this material to transform their very persons, so that it becomes a primary lens through which they view the world and their role in it. Religious should devote their lives to zeal for their mission. Whether contemplative or active, religious need to embrace their institute's self-definition and actively promote it to one another and to those outside. As with the other six concrete actions mentioned above, persevering in an institute's charism and mission requires its members to act in a balanced fashion.

These observations list only some of ways in which religious can persevere in their vocational commitments. They are extensive enough, however, to indicate the direction their reflections should take on this important virtue. If nothing else, they demonstrate the complexity of the subject and offer initial suggestions for helping religious remain faithful to Christ to the very end.

Conclusion

Perseverance in religious life requires individuals and the community to recommit themselves daily to the vows and to community life. This virtue needs to be cultivated at every juncture, be it postulancy, novitiate, active ministry, or retirement. Doing so means asking for God's help, cooperating with the graces received, implementing appropriate practices that will make it a shared communal value, and seeking new ways to encourage each other to carry on the work of the Lord.

As they seek to persevere in their vocations, religious would do well to listen to the voice of moderation. On the practical level, in their rules, structures, practices, lifestyle, and orientation toward the world they should avoid the extremes of softness and obstinacy. They should also view their vocations in terms of their entire sojourn through life. This means examining their circumstances and making appropriate adaptations in keeping with the purpose or charism of their religious institute, their own needs, and those of the local community.

Most importantly, religious should recognize how perseverance is an expression of courage. Martyrdom for the faith may be the highest expression of Christian fortitude, but perseverance in one's calling is not very far behind. Following Christ in the radical way of a religious vocation demands hard work and sacrifice. It seeks to draw the best out of people and enable them to commit themselves in ways they never thought possible. To give of oneself in small, genuine, and heartfelt ways over the course of an entire lifetime is no easy charge. To do so, religious need to ask every day of their lives for the patience, constancy, and hope they need to fulfill the plan God has for them.

Reflection Questions

What value does perseverance have in responding to a person's call in life? How does it relate to the virtue of courage? How does it relate to the vows of poverty, chastity, and obedience? What value does it have for life in community? What does it signify for religious, whose state of life has been associated with Christian martyrdom? Has your religious community discussed the need for perseverance in the various aspects of its communal life? What concrete steps can you take to emphasize its importance for your religious community?

Epilogue

By following the Catholic Church's clear and extensive teaching on the spirituality of communion, religious communities can narrow the gap between what they profess and their actual lived experience. A good, hard look at the causes of this gap can help them develop constructive ways of dealing with it.

Forming Proper Attitudes

Psychological terms that describe human behavior — *action, habit*, and *attitude* — can be applied usefully to religious life. An *action* involves a single deliberated object and intention. A *good habit*, as opposed to a bad habit, is an active pattern of constructive behavior established by constant repetition. An *attitude* is an active habit (disposition) voluntarily acquired by repeatedly opting for the fundamental values behind a person's life project.

An action is singular and concrete; a voluntary disposition is a deeply rooted, deliberated pattern of behavior; an attitude is an ingrained preference for a particular set of values.[1] An individual, for example, may participate at

---

1. This description of the action, voluntary disposition, and attitude comes from Fabio Giardini, *Pray without Ceasing: Toward a Systematic Psychotheology of Christian Prayerlife* (Leominster/Rome: Gracewing/Millennium, 1998), 363–66.

Sunday Mass as an isolated event (goes rarely, if ever), as a good habit (always attends), or as the expression of a deeply held attitude (obedience to the commandments, desire to give glory and honor to God). In the ideal world, actions, good habits, and attitudes reinforce each other, and are strong and constant. In real life, however, such continuity varies, or even breaks down. This discontinuity or breakdown happens with the actions, habits, and attitudes of families, groups, or religious communities.

By shaping their attitudes in light of the Church's teaching on the spirituality of communion, religious communities can make their lived experience consistent with their vision. They can begin by recognizing the reciprocal relationship among actions, habits, and the formation of attitudes. Attitudes give rise to actions and habits, while at the same time being shaped by them. Acknowledging these relationships is the foundation for the formation of consecrated persons whose actions are consistent with the values they truly hold and which define their life's project.

This reciprocal relationship among actions, voluntary dispositions, and attitudes provides religious communities a way of developing strategies to connect their vision with their lived experience. To identify and clarify its defining vision, the community — as individuals and together — must reflect on the interrelationship among their teachings, structures, and practices in an ongoing process of nuancing (and perhaps redefining) their vision in order to express what they truly believe. Next, the members need to express this defining vision in their daily lives through concrete structures and practices. These structures and practices need to be firm yet flexible, taking into account the Church's three fundamental principles of right relationships: the dignity of the human person, the common good, and the virtue of solidarity.

Values that support life in a religious community include service, hospitality, unconditional love, universality, and benevolence.[2] Single actions or good habits acquired by repetition lead to a deep, grace-filled, yet fully human embrace of such principles and values. Both vision and experience, in other words, are rooted in a commonly expressed determination to persist in walking the way of the Lord Jesus. They also flow from communal structures that foster an authentic sharing of both mind and heart. Such structures should be carefully planned, rooted in tradition, and regularly appraised to insure their relevance in a community's current context.[3]

Communities of consecrated life can be effective instruments of the spirituality of communion by inculcating the basic values of right relationship among their members. Doing so promotes an ever-increasing unity between vision and lived experience.

Vision and Reality

A religious institution has a public life and a private life; it can also have a secret life.[4] A common vision and lived reality requires communities of consecrated life to consider carefully why they ask their members to think or act in the ways they do, so that the public face which the outside world sees corresponds to the private life lived within the community. Not achieving this correspondence can generate a secret life known only to a select few, hidden even from members, institutionally suppressed and even denied. Such a secret life can gen-

---

2. These last five values are developed in Ciardi, *Koinonia*, 323–31.

3. See the section, "Teaching Methods for the Life of Unity," in Ibid., 331–36.

4. For the distinction between public, private, and secret lives, see Robert Fulghum, *Maybe (Maybe Not): Second Thoughts from a Secret Life* (New York: Villard, 1993), 7–8.

erate dysfunction within a community and cause misery for both the members and those they wish to serve.

To live in right relationship with themselves and with others, members need to acknowledge and understand all the facets of their common life — public, private, and secret — and deal with them maturely and responsibly. Otherwise, a gap can open between vision and lived experience, leaving the community to live in a "house of mirrors" based on mere appearances. A religious community needs to explore its shadow side, the aspects of communal experience that influence conscious decisions but are perceived by members only peripherally. By acknowledging that such a secret life exists and by making everyone aware of it, a community comes to understand itself and can channel its resources in creative and constructive ways.

What does this mean concretely for the life of a religious community? Although the Church's teaching on the relationship among the constituent elements of the consecrated life — community life and the three evangelical counsels — has been adequately presented elsewhere,[5] still more is required. When examining its spirituality (on the congregational, provincial, or local levels), each religious community needs to examine whether its vision of life in community and the vows corresponds to its lived experience. When doing so, it needs to determine whether any gap between vision and experience is increasing or decreasing, and whether progress is being made to bridge it. It should do the same concerning its vision of its charism and its actual lived experience, as well its understanding and practice of the spirituality of communion.

5. See, for example, Ciardi, *Koinonia*, 336–39. See also Dennis J. Billy, *Evangelical Kernels: A Theological Spirituality of Religious Life* (Staten Island, NY: Alba House, 1993). In the latter, I explain the fundamental principle of fifteen theological disciplines and develop their significance for the evangelical counsels and community life.

Conclusion: Living in the Gap

By living "in the gap," experts in communion learn how to narrow it and eventually eliminate it. In this respect, the importance of the eschatological and countercultural qualities of consecrated life becomes apparent. By bridging the gap between vision and reality, consecrated persons affirm the "already-but-not-yet" quality of even the best human relationships. By striving to narrow the discrepancy between the two, they affirm God's presence in their midst and witness to those around them a value-based life oriented toward realizing the kingdom. This juxtaposition of the eschatological and the countercultural makes consecrated life both a challenge and a consolation to those who seek communion and right relationship with themselves, others, and God.

In the end, all religious must ponder and respond to some challenging questions. They must allow God's Spirit to sweep across the deep, dark waters of their human frailties like a mighty wind so that it can form bonds of authentic human love that are the foundations of a new creation. They must allow the Spirit to knock down the walls of envy, hatred, and jealousy that can divide and isolate in order to build up a communion of living persons who live and move and have their being in the communion of the living God. They must put off the old self and put on the new by espousing attitudes toward one another befitting consecrated persons called to be disciples of Christ and true experts in communion. Ultimately, it comes down to making choices, again and again, day after day, in the very warp and woof of life — until it comes out right.

Appendix

The Objective Superiority of Religious Life?

Pope John Paul II's apostolic exhortation on the consecrated life, *Vita consecrata*, has been criticized for using language that seems to place the vowed life above other states of life in the Church. Two passages in particular have generated intense comment: the statement in number 18, "Christian tradition has always spoken of the *objective superiority of the consecrated life*"; and a related claim in number 32, "As a way of showing forth the Church's holiness, *it is to be recognized that the consecrated life ... has an objective superiority*" (italics in originals). For some, such language represents a return to a two-tiered mentality that privileges the consecrated life in the Church and belittles the worth of other Christian callings. They think that speaking of the "objective superiority" of the consecrated life implies that the laity and clergy occupy a second-class status in the Church. Such criticism notes that Vatican II documents consciously avoided such potentially polarizing language and, when referring to the consecrated life, characterized it as a deepening of the baptismal commitment or as a way of being joined to the mystery of the Church "in a special way" (e.g., *LG*, 44).

Explanations

Three explanations have been advanced that minimize the significance of this language. The first considers the document as the final product of a long synodal process during which vying theologies of the consecrated life were expressed and, where possible, integrated into a single but possibly compromised statement. According to this reasoning, the phrase "objective superiority" represents a minority opinion that was "slipped in" to pacify vocal conservative elements at the synod. Since many hands go into the writing of such a document, so the argument goes, this editorial concession could have easily made its way into the final draft. Moreover, the theological significance of that phrase diminishes when read in light of the entire document.

A second interpretation focuses on subtle differences in translation. The document, most likely, was first written in Italian and then translated into Latin and a number of other languages. The English version translates the Italian "obiettiva eccellenza" as "objective superiority." Some claim that "eccellenza" and its Latin equivalent "excellentia" are softer than the English "superiority," and do not intend the two-tiered connotation that the English translation conveys. According to this interpretation, the English version has a theological slant not present in the original Italian and the derived Latin versions. A more precise translation would be "objective excellence" rather than "objective superiority."

A final explanation examines the level of authority associated with an apostolic exhortation. According to this opinion, Vatican II's deliberate turn from a two-tiered mentality includes a paradigmatic shift in theological language regarding the consecrated life. A papal exhortation is said to have lesser authority, and so cannot displace theological changes set in place by an ecumenical council. As a result, if a magisterial document uses language that is inconsistent with Vatican II teaching, the authority of the council takes precedence. Referring to the "objective superiority" of the consecrated life is considered one such instance.

The responses to these explanations demonstrate a range of reactions to John Paul's exhortation. Opponents of the first argument assert that, minority opinion or not, the pope approved the final draft of the document, since it bears his name; no one else can claim authorship. Even if he sought the help of others to compose it, and even if minority opinions were listened to and incorporated into the final draft, John Paul II approved such language in the document and considers it to be in fundamental continuity with the theology of Vatican II.

Those who dismiss the second argument point out that at least one authoritative dictionary (*Il grande dizionario Garzanti*) defines "eccellenza" as "superiorità assoluta" ("absolute superiority") and that in English "objective superiority" makes much more literary and aesthetic sense than "objective excellence." Even if "objective superiority" is not the best possible translation of "obiettiva eccellenza," it remains in the approved English version of *Vita consecrata* and must be considered authoritative unless it is officially changed.

Critics of the third argument point out that the Magisterium interprets prior magisterial statements in the light of current circumstances and that, by using such language, the exhortation is taking into account the fact that "In recent years, theological reflection on the nature of the consecrated life has deepened the new insights which emerged from the teaching of the Second Vatican Council" (*VC*, 29). According to this scenario, John Paul II is exercising his ordinary teaching function to convey how understanding of the consecrated life has been elaborated and deepened since the Council.

An Alternative Reading

These arguments — those who object to the language and those who support it — focus on the precise meaning, placement, and authority of the phrase "objectivity superiority" but overlook the exhortation's nuances concerning the place of the consecrated life in the life of the Church. When examined in this larger context, "objective superiority" can be understood not as the reintroduction of a two-tiered mentality, but as a careful assertion of how the consecrated life *"indisputably belongs to the life and holiness of the Church"* (*LG*, 44; *VC*, 29). Simply stated, such language does *not* reveal the reintroduction of a two-tiered mentality. An examination of its use in context bears this out.

To start with, the exhortation presents the teachings of Vatican II as "an enlightening point of reference for subsequent doctrinal developments" (*VC*, 13). It points out that, although the Council "emphasized the profound reality of ecclesial communion ... in recent years there has been felt the need to clarify *the specific identity of the various states of life*, their vocation and their particular mission in the Church" (*VC*, 4). While recognizing the common dignity that all the faithful share by virtue of their baptism (see *VC*, 31), the exhortation acknowledges the movement of the Spirit, who "establishes the Church as an organic communion in the diversity of vocations, charisms, and ministries" (*VC*, 31). Within this context, all three states of life have a clear role to play in the Church: "[T]he lay faithful have as their specific but not exclusive characteristic, activity in the world; the clergy, ministry;

consecrated men and women, special conformity to Christ, chaste, poor and obedient" (*VC*, 31).

The exhortation, moreover, employs the imagery of light to emphasize the fundamental unity of the lay, priestly, and consecrated states. These vocations are "like so many rays of the one light of Christ, whose radiance 'brightens the countenance of the Church' " (*VC*, 16). Each state shines forth and reflects in its own special way the honor and glory of God. The secular character of the laity reflects the mystery of the Incarnate Word as the Alpha and Omega of the world. As living images of Christ the Head and Shepherd, sacred ministers guide the people of God as they await his coming in glory. By conforming their whole existence to Christ, consecrated persons "show that the Incarnate Son of God is the eschatological goal towards which all things tend" (*VC*, 16).

This fundamental eschatological orientation expresses the *radical* nature of consecrated life. For this reason, the consecrated life — one of the Church's essential and characteristic elements — expresses the very nature of the Church (see *VC*, 29). It is in this context that the "objective superiority" of the consecrated life must be understood. Even though it was chosen by Jesus himself and represents "the most radical way of living the Gospel on this earth" (*VC*, 18), the consecrated life is *not* objectively superior to other states of life *in all respects*. The context of these phrases shows that the exhortation considers the consecrated life "objectively superior" primarily "as a way of *showing forth* the Church's holiness" (*VC*, 32). By virtue of the eschatological nature of the vows and the common life, consecrated persons remind themselves and others of the universal call to holiness. Their mission "is to remind their brothers and sisters to keep their eyes fixed on the peace which is to come, and to strive for the definitive happiness found in God" (*VC*, 33). The life they have been called to live is especially suited to this type of witness.

The discussion does not end here. The same logic can be used to demonstrate an "objective superiority" of the lay state when it comes to bringing the Good News into the market place (see *VC*, 16, 31) or the "objective superiority" of the clerical state when it comes to shepherding the flock of Christ (see *VC*, 16, 31). Such terminology does not represent a reversion to the two-tiered mentality common up to the time of the Second Vatican Council. In fact, when viewed in the context of the theological nuances and levels of discourse found in the exhortation, a good case can be made that such language demonstrates the exact opposite. It highlights, in other words, the specific function of the consecrated life in the Church as a radical, eschatological witness to the call to holiness. In the post-Vatican II theology of the consecrated life, "objective superiority" refers not to a state of *being*, but to a *function*.

Conclusion

The phrase "objective superiority" appears only twice in *Vita consecrata*: once when referring to its use in Christian tradition (see *VC*, 18); the other when pointing out a specific function of consecrated life (see *VC*, 32). Taking these two references out of context and implying that they represent a return to a mentality that relegates other states of life in the Church to second-class status misrepresents the theology of the consecrated life expressed in the document as a whole. Other phrases in *Vita consecrata* that refer to "mutual relationships" (*VC*, 31) "common dignity" (*VC*, 31) and "equal dignity" (*VC*, 31) among the faithful clearly refute such an interpretation.

Reading the document in context shows that the phrase "objective superiority" delineates the consecrated life's specific task—to offer radical, eschatological testimony of the coming of the kingdom. At one time in the Church's history such witness was closely tied to a mentality of first-class and second-class citizenry. The Second Vatican Council rejected this mentality and emphasizes the universal call to holiness and the common bond that joins all Christians by virtue of their baptismal commitment. *Vita consecrata* introduces the language, but not the mentality, in a particular context as a way to describe the unique function of the consecrated life in "showing forth the Church's holiness" (*VC*, 32). To put it another way, for much of the Church's history the language of superiority reflected a two-tiered mentality; with the Second Vatican Council, the mentality and the language of superiority were melted down and recast as theological categories (the People of God, the universal call to holiness) that embody the Church more accurately for a new age. *Vita consecrata* has reintroduced the language of superiority so as to clarify and even deepen those insights of the Second Vatican Council.

Acknowledgements

All quotations from Scripture come from *Holy Bible: The New Revised Standard Version with Apocrypha* (New York, Oxford: Oxford University Press, 1989). Earlier versions of material in this book have appeared elsewhere under the following titles: "Right Relationships in Consecrated Life," *Review for Religious* 61(2002): 494–510 [Introduction and Epilogue]; "Religious Life and Conversion Language," *Review for Religious* 52(1993): 806–16 [Chapter One]; "*Vita Consecrata* and the Anthropology of the Vows," *Review for Religious* 58(1999): 384–92 [Chapter Two]; "Called to Community," *Review for Religious* 54(1995): 371–82 [Chapter Three]; "*Vita Consecrata* and the Spirituality of Communion," *Dominican Ashram* 15(no. 4, 1996): 172–85 [Chapter Four]; "Virtue and Community Structures," *Dominican Ashram* 18(no. 2, 1999): 84–95 [Chapter Five]; "The Courage to Persist: Perseverance in Religious Life," *Review for Religious* 62(2003): 72–82 [Chapter Six]; "'Objective Superiority' in *Vita Consecrata*," *Review for Religious* 55(1996): 640–45 [Appendix].

I would like to extend a special word of thanks to Gary Brandl, Publisher; Tom Masters, Editorial Director; and Julie James, Director of Marketing and Sales at New City Press for their invaluable help at every stage in the evaluation, preparation, and distribution of this book.

Available by the same author:

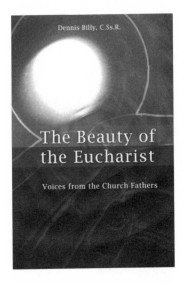

The Beauty of the Eucharist
Voices from the Church Fathers
Dennis Billy, C.Ss.R.
ISBN 978-1-56548-328-6, 252 pages

"This is a wonderful and user-friendly introduction to Patristic writing about the Eucharist.... The book would be extremely useful in an introductory course on the sacraments in a seminary setting or for an adult education series in a parish. The chapters are very succinct and the exposition is clear and lucid.... A book that introduces a wide audience to foundational Christian reflection on the Eucharist that is at once theological, biblical, devotional, and pastoral is to be welcomed."

Rev. Dr. Leander S. Harding, *The Living Church*

Call Toll Free (in the U.S.) 1-800-462-5980 or 1-845-229-0335
www.newcitypress.com